CW01034460

The 'mean streets' of New York, Los Angeles and Chicago have dominated American crime fiction from Raymond Chandler and Dashiell Hammett to Sara Paretsky and *Blade Runner*. Like Marlowe and V. I. Warshawski before him, Ralph Willett undertakes a one-man investigation into the dangerous realms of urban American detective fiction, uncovering clues to their hold in the popular imagination, text by text and city by city.

On the one hand, a menacing labyrinth or urban jungle; on the other, a bohemian and exotic space, the American city is the site of many distinctly modern anxieties to do with gender, race, affluence, poverty, urbanisation and technology. 'The opaque complexity of modern city life is represented by crime' (Raymond Williams) and the detective, or investigating cop, emerges as the man (or woman as the case may be) who endeavours to solve crime and, at the same time, explain the city.

Through a close analysis of films as well as popular fiction, Ralph Willett explores an imaginative geography of the modern American city: a place of opportunity and desire as well as murder and lawlessness.

Ralph Willett is Senior Fellow at the University of Hull

FRONT COVER ILLUSTRATION: Todd Elkin, 1994
courtesy *The Voice Literary Supplement*, New York

THE NAKED CITY

URBAN CRIME FICTION
IN THE USA

Ralph Willett

Manchester University Press
Manchester and New York

distributed exclusively in the USA and Canada by St. Martin's Press

Copyright © Ralph Willett 1996

Ralph Willett asserts the moral right
to be identified as the author of this work

Published by Manchester University Press
Oxford Road, Manchester M13 9NR, UK
and Room 400, 175 Fifth Avenue, New York, NY 10010, USA

Distributed exclusively in the USA and Canada
by St. Martin's Press, Inc. 175 Fifth Avenue, New York, NY 10010, USA

British Library Cataloguing-in-Publication Data
A catalogue record is available from the British Library

Library of Congress Cataloging-in-Publication Data
Willett, Ralph
    The naked city : urban crime fiction in the USA / Ralph Willett
        p. c.m.
    Includes bibliographical references and index
    ISBN 0-7190-4300-X. — ISBN 0-7190-4301-8 (alk. paper)
        1. Detective and mystery stories. American—History and criticism.
    2. American fiction—20th century—History and criticism. 3. City
    and town life in literature. 4. Cities and towns in literature.
    5. Criminals in literature. 6. Crime in literature. I. Title.
    PS374.D4W55 1996
    813'087209321732—dc20   95-35843
                                                              CIP

ISBN 0 7190 4300 X *hardback*
ISBN 0 7190 4301 8 *paperback*

First published 1996
00 99 98 97 96   10 9 8 7 6 5 4 3 2 1

Typeset in Aldus
by Koinonia, Manchester
Printed in Great Britain
by Bell & Bain Ltd, Glasgow

In memoriam
ERIC MOTTRAM
TEACHER AND FRIEND
1924–1995

CONTENTS

ACKNOWLEDGEMENTS

Professor Brian Rigby was in the right place at the right time; his wise suggestions were of immeasurable assistance in composing the introduction. Professor Brian Lee kindly read the chapter on film; I believe its structure is more acceptable after revisions which he helped to instigate. Dr Dave Sibley showed me his current work on Chicago which kept up my momentum as I approached the relevant chapter. At the Brynmor Jones Library, University of Hull, the staff were, as they have been over the years, unfailingly helpful, especially Ruth Ireland and Pauline Dennison. Study leave granted by the University of Hull in 1993 put me in touch with materials unavailable or difficult to access in the UK. In the USA, Fran Jowett and Brian Richardson in Virginia spurred my interest in Miami and its crime fiction, Kay Mussell at American University, Washington, DC dealt reliably and genially with a series of scholarly requests, and Barbara G. Peters at The Poisoned Pen Bookstore, Scottsdale, Arizona kept me supplied with texts and, through her remarkable *Booknews*, much invaluable information. Don Blackburn in Hull and Christopher Brookeman in London were both sources of those vital commodities: spirited discussion and light relief. As always, Jean Willett supplied good sense, support, wit and affection in abundance. At Manchester University Press Anita Roy constantly encouraged me and provided helpful suggestions. The completion of this book was overshadowed by the sudden death of Professor Eric Mottram, an inspiration to generations of American Studies students. Taking into account his essays on Ross Macdonald, guns in America, and cars in movies, I see now that the text can stand as a suitable tribute and as an expression of gratitude.

1 *Introduction*

URBAN DISCOURSE

The investigation of American cities by cultural analysts has been both retrospective and present-oriented. They have shared a common desire to explore the various significances of the modern city and to acknowledge and engage with the work of earlier 'students' of the urban environment.

Thus the nature of such projects is multi-disciplinary, embracing in various combinations, architectural and social history, semiotics, the visual arts, politics and, for the present purpose, popular literature. The exploration of the city as a modern phenomenon determined by mass society has an established history so that writers such as Marshall Berman and Christopher Prendergast who focus on the nineteenth century are able to demonstrate continuities with and differences from the twentieth century. One of those differences is the shift in relative importance from the European city (specifically Paris) to the American, initially New York, more recently Los Angeles: 'The distinctive sign of nineteenth-century urbanism was the boulevard, a medium for bringing explosive material and human forces together; the hallmark of twentieth-century urbanism has been the highway, a means for putting them asunder.'[1]

Berman's last phrase already implies some of the relevant factors in the modernist anatomy of the city, achieved by the process known as reading or mapping the city: space, movement, functionality, fragmentation, disruption. Further it is in establishing the relation between human and material forces that the mutually defining concept of identity is clarified. The question of identity, in the case of the urban conglomeration and its inhabitants, individually and collectively, has been an obsession since the nineteenth century, often indicating the difficulty of making sense of the modern city. That difficulty may impinge on the detective in his or her search for selfhood. On returning to New Orleans, Dave Robicheaux, in James Lee Burke's *A Morning For Flamingos* (1990) concludes that his only identity would be in the reflections he saw in the eyes of others.

T. S. Eliot's anti-romantic vision, in *The Waste Land*, of London commuters as a melancholy procession of morose automata is a celebrated and characteristic modernist image, echoed in Fritz Lang's film *Metropolis* and Elmer Rice's play *The Adding Machine*. The repetition of 'flowed' to describe the crowd's action contributes to the representation of modern urban society as a faceless, undifferentiated, swirling mass or, in Zola's phrase, a black swarm. All too quickly, this version of the city as fluid and amorphous invites the perception that the city defies understanding and is too enigmatic or too compact with information to be intelligible. To regard the city as unreadable, an impenetrable blur, is to ignore distinctions of gender, class, race and economic status. Certain editions of this viewpoint which emphasise the dizzying, disruptive speed of urban life argue for a contemporary response which dispenses with observation and control in favour of floating through the city, numb yet euphoric.

In the early part of the twentieth century a new technological source of information appeared: already electrification in American cities was such as to make them significantly brighter than their European counterparts. Electricity simplified for the viewer the mapping of the city literally highlighting landmarks and important locations. As ribbons of light major streets formed abstract patterns, some joined by the bright loops of bridges. The modern city was also energetically commercial as electric signs advertised leading products; conversely, the dazzling spectacle of the city at night mythicised the drab daytime metropolis and effectively obliterated less affluent, unlit areas of the city. Their lesser importance indicated by blankness, these dark patches, denying instant information and knowledge, would become part of the discourse of hard-boiled fiction and its filmic equivalents.

The best known figure in the study of modern urban experience is the *flâneur*, a mythological ideal-type found more in discourse than in everyday life. As masterfully interpreted by Walter Benjamin, the *flâneur* is, on the one hand, an observant classifier of the city's population 'who reads people's characters not only from the physiognomy of their faces but via a social physiognomy of the streets';[2] and, on the other, a dandyish connoisseur of metropolitan pleasures and delights, increasingly the offerings of a commercial culture. Celebrated in the work of Balzac and later Baudelaire, he provides a surrogate for the watchful (male) detective of popular fiction, one who listens, searches and above all, like the private 'eye', sees and deciphers the signifiers of that labyrinth of populated spaces and buildings which forms the modern metropolis – strange and menacing but also intoxicating. Benjamin claims that whatever track the *flâneur* as hunter follows will lead him to a crime.

It is the 'philosophical stroller' moving through but retaining a distance from modern urban delights who aestheticises the city and envisages it as pure spectacle, a unifying vision derived from the panorama. This quest for visual intelligibility has a different significance in hard-boiled fiction where the solution of a crime brings with it the knowledge of duplicity and corruption, clarifying the social morphology of the imagined city.

Benjamin also came to realise that social and political consequences could ensue from the movement of history. In the *Passagen-Werk* of the late 1920s, he interprets the objects of city life (walls, newspapers, letterboxes) as the empowering possessions of the urban masses including the unemployed, memorably photographed by Brassai. In the late 1930s, Benjamin finds that the *flâneur* alone inhabits the streets, and the walls become semiotically the *flâneur's* desk; his role is reduced to that of urban reporter, the journalist/writer as 'sandwich man', informing or persuading on behalf of the state.

The representation of the modern city as coherent, ordered and stable draws upon urban theorists, especially the French (Henri Lefebvre and the two Michels, Foucault and de Certeau), whose baleful critiques postulate a world of regulated spaces, controlled by supervision and manipulation. Alexander Haagen's shopping centres in the Afro-American areas of Los Angeles, both inner city – South Central – and suburban – Baldwin Hills – are the modern equivalent of Bentham's panopticon, with security and surveillance the chief priorities. A fictional version is provided in Elmore Leonard's Atlantic City novel *Glitz* (1985): the action on the floor of Spade's casino is observed elsewhere by an Eye in the Sky surveillance system, a multitude of screens which provides an image for Leonard's style in a novel which contains 113 shifts of scene. As surveillance becomes a feature of crime novels and films, the suggestion implied is that it is absent from the 'everyday ' existence of realistic, slice-of-life novels.

De Certeau shared this version of the city as organised space, using the term 'quadrillage', meaning both close surveillance by state forces and the squared pattern of graph paper and modern streets. However his utopian vision of pedestrians writing an urban text they do not read challenges the concept of panoptic power: 'The city ... is no longer a theatre for programmed, controlled operations. Beneath the discourses ideologizing it... there is a proliferation of tricks and fusions of power ... that are without rational clarity - impossible to manage.'[3]

Although the grid system with its uniformity and rationality can be viewed as empowering, holding exotic architecture in check or enabling the individual to grasp and possess mentally the shape of the city, the charge that the grid is soulless and monotonous remains compelling. Consequently, older areas of Manhattan settled before the geometric plan was implemented, have been especially prized. Their curves, spaces and interstices provide those cracks in the public sector of cities celebrated by current theorists, though their corners however quaint would still facilitate voyeuristic scrutinising. Increasingly, the panoptic gaze is giving rise to the cyborg gaze, or self-scrutiny. We watch ourselves as someone else in a third person narrative.

Lefebvre's passive consumers and observers may simply experience bewilderment as a result of the pace of twentieth century city life; Georg Simmel has referred to the exhausted nerves of city dwellers, indicating a neurotic reaction to the velocity and standardisation of industrial and commercial activity. Bewilderment is also the perceived response to the speed and volume of circulation, the flow of people, money (a source of tension as well as fascination), and vehicles. Here also there are implications for control, intelligibility and representation as sections of Dos Passos's panoramic novel *USA* (1938) testify. Nor should it be forgotten that while the character of the city as portrayed in crime fiction is dangerous, violent and squalid, the metropolis is also the site of opportunity, aspiration and success.

The circulation of bodies since the nineteenth century has been governed by political philosophy based on notions of class and social stability. Keeping the city 'clean' has assumed symbolic significance in the idea of the lower depths, associated with the lumpenproletariat, the recognisable exterior of the forces that exist and emerge from below. Bourgeois imperatives sought to control dangerous elements in the urban population by keeping them out of sight. Distinguished geographically from the 'healthy' respectable working class, marginalised groups (criminals, beggars, prostitutes) were stigmatised by images of disease, fuelling an alarmed discourse, prioritising the protection (by separation) of the wholesome and productive sectors of society. Thus the catacombs and sewers of the city become in nineteenth-century French fiction the world of the savage, the sub-human and the excremental.

By the 1870s in New York, 'dive' which originally meant a disreputable drinking place usually in a basement, had, among detectives, become a term for any foul or criminal place. The lower depths/disease metaphor extends readily into the era of mass culture, and images in Hollywood movies, especially *film noir*, suggested a process of irrigation and hygienic street-cleaning, a flushing out of the city's bowels. The discourse of film magazines in the 1930s, while associating gangsters with the tawdry neon glamour of the cities, portrayed them as reptiles and sewer rats, hideously diseased. In 'No Blue Skies'(1968) an episode of TV's *Hawaii Five-O*, Joey, a night club singer and thief shot by the police, assumes he has chosen the right place to die: a hotel's underground car park.

Circulation has other material meanings notably modes of transport and traffic, which the detective enters of necessity, his profession demanding action and movement especially the exploration of the city by car. In Loren D. Estelman's *Sweet Women Lie* (1990), Amos Walker, a Detroit detective, alludes to the components of the city's industrial image: assembly lines and automobile plants. On the one hand this recognition influences Walker's semiotic reading of the city: to him the Ford auditorium in the Civic Center looks 'a little like an air filter'. On the other, Chapter 17 finds the PI (private investigator) in Dearborn, the heart of the Ford empire where he takes the opportunity to record the arrival of black immigrants in Dearborn in 1914 and the racism they encountered. In the previous chapter, he expressed his desire for the power and mobility ('shrieking into deep space') symbolised by the car, even the ancient gas-guzzling Mercury he currently drives. As he cruises old city streets to meditate on a case, his mood sinks to melancholy and nostalgia for he arrives at Outer Drive, once the boundary of the city limits 'before the developers ... began a fifteen mile crawl northward, devouring trees and grass as they went and dropping concrete and asphalt behind them like manure' .[4]

The culture of transport, then, constitutes another unifying yet bewildering network of associations, one which facilitates commodity circulation and exchange, as Benjamin announced in his Arcades project. Yet the facilitation of circulation cannot be regarded solely as a positive aid to mapping the city. Prendergast exposes the paradox that 'the clearer, cleaner and more uniform the city came to appear physically, the more opaque and mysterious it came to seem socially as governed by a contingent play of forces, transactions and interests'. So the modernist undertaking of supplanting cluttered interiors and the unhealthy structures of the nineteenth century with light, airy buildings and roof gardens was ambiguous in its results.

Just as the houses which fascinate Anthony Vidler in *The Architectural Uncanny* (1992) survey the occupants with silent menace, and, it can be added, the commodities in shop windows survey the customers, so the hard flat light cultivated in the postmodern city contributes to the city walker's feelings of drift and risk. Mystery, confusion, and frenetic ferment – these can fuel paranoia insofar as 'it may be ... that what truly controls the city ... seeks to remain hidden, unlocatable, at once fluid and disoriginated'.[5] The kind of narrative this implies is frequently a feature of the American hard-boiled novel in which the investigator's role is to reveal whatever the city conceals: secret passions, liaisons, crimes and corruptions. As early as the end of the nineteenth century, the significance of the urban detective lay in the fact that, as Raymond Williams observed in *The Country and the City*, he was the man who could find his way through the fog and 'penetrate the intricacies of the streets'. Like the *flâneur*, and the hitman in Luc Besson's film *Leon* (1994), his spectatorship of the city must be secret, undetected. For this reason Besson set his film not in Paris but New York where, he has claimed, no one is interested in the activities of others.

To identify the reification of the city (as dirt, disease or garbage, for example) is one way of becoming aware that perceptions of the urban landscape are mediated by means of representations, through the processes of reading, describing, naming. Literature and film in particular (and more recently TV) have participated, through interacting signifying practices, in a dialectic with the material world which renders such oppositions as reality/fiction and authentic/fake inapplicable. The 'real' city merges with what Robert Warshow has famously called the dangerous, sad city of the imagination. 'History', distinct from fiction but still a species of narrative, increasingly appears as one text among many.

The city generates texts and also functions as text, one characterised by intertextuality, intangible relationships and instability. Our representations of the American city, despite its apparent newness, are vulnerable to physical changes. Jean Paul Sartre noted in 1946 that New York already had not only historical monuments but ruins; later, Marshall Berman described it as 'a Baudelairean forest of symbols' but one 'where axes and bulldozers are always at work, and great works constantly crashing down; where new meanings are forever springing up with and falling down from the constructed trees'.[6] Buildings resembling those in the film *The Naked City* (1946) were being demolished to make space for the new United Nations building as the film was being shot, and in Paul Auster's metaphysical detective novel, *City of Glass* (1985), Quinn registers a sense of impermanence generated by the rate of urban change in New York. Sarah Schulman's second novel, *Girls, Visions and Everything* (1986) also represents the urban landscape in terms of instability, making this a reason for walking the streets as a practice of resistance and possession: 'if you settle in your own little hole, she'll change so fast that by the time you wake up, she won't be yours anymore... '.[7]

Historically, the hard-boiled novel has fostered a recognisably colloquial American verbal style, avoiding what Jim Collins in *Uncommon Cultures* calls semantic imperialism in favour of a shared discourse, one with which readers are familiar or which they are willing to learn. It is a language suited to the fast, aggressive modern world of the city, able to record spatial contrasts, the social symbolism of grids and interstices, reactions to new technologies and consumer styles, ambivalence towards apartment life, the strains of class and ethnic difference, and the existential experience of tenements, mean streets and slums.

Conventional hard-boiled language is terse, laconic, acerbic and witty. One of its enduring techniques, adopted recently by female PIs, is the wisecrack, a stylised demonstration of knowledge which expresses an irreverence towards authority and institutional power. Wisecracks put to use as weapons are an assertion of autonomy, a defiant refusal to be browbeaten. They introduce an unsettling element into the interplay of speech modes as a strategy in the quest for meanings and solutions.

In novels written in the last quarter of a century, urban

types such as detectives, criminals, lawyers and politicos are often linked by their own language. As professionals sharing information and undergoing similar experiences, they need their own 'business' discourse. Wisecracks, slang and general verbal toughness are the means of ordering and interpreting events, marking the investigator out from the crowd, enabling him/her to function effectively in the anonymous urban milieu. Furthermore, since the city is a body of customs and traditions, access to information and records (the written depository of memory) bestows knowledge and control, as the crime-in-the-city narrative reveals.

That power is limited, Scott R. Christianson has argued, since the narrative represents the process of making meaning as a struggle. The detective all too frequently achieves only partial understanding or flawed justice. Thus the texts of detective fiction can be used deconstructively to display the fragmentation and complexity of modern life and to undermine the tendency of narrative to achieve control and closure. Such novels tend towards the feelings of melancholy, regret and emptiness suggested by such titles as: *The Big Sleep* (1938), *The Long Goodbye* (1953), *The Last Good Kiss* (1978).

Christianson understands the language of hard-boiled fiction to be unitary, and numerous texts can be cited in which the voice of the PI is monologically in control. While hard-boiled vernacular language is frequently dominant, as in Ed McBain's novels where characters speak alike, it can also be found competing with other languages in the same text. Literature in the USA has been a clash of voices as diverse as the overlapping groups and subgroups of the city. Walter Mosley, the contemporary black Jewish novelist has explicitly identified the two languages in his thrillers – black dialect and Chandler's street language of fear. Texts as different as Robert Parker's *A Catskill Eagle* (1983), Ishmael Reed's *Mumbo Jumbo* (1972) and K. C. Constantine's *Always a Body to Trade* (1983) show how Afro-American discourse can challenge the notion of a unitary language system. Street talk in hard-boiled fiction emerges as the privileged voice in contestation with other modes of expression: the cynical misanthropy of Harlan Potter in Raymond Chandler's *The Long Goodbye*, the smooth, devious, clubman's rhetoric of Casper Gutman in Dashiell Hammett's *The Maltese Falcon* (1930). or the nervous sanctimony of Meade Alexander, undermined by Spenser ('I like it, I eat French crap a lot') at a classy restaurant in Robert B. Parker's *The Widening Gyre* (1983).

The wit and wisecracking are retained in sharp and abrasive street speech, shaping obscenity into rhythmic patterns and often blackly comic. In the novels of George V. Higgins, the aspiration of the narrative towards discursive authority is checked by other people's stories. Elsewhere, *Always a Body to Trade* sets different verbal styles side by side within the discourse of law and policing to establish levels of experience and ignorance. The police chief Balzic and the Deputy US Attorney Feinstein, engaged in the trading of the novel's title, operate pragmatically: 'For God's sake, man, what the hell do you think the law is all about? It's trade, it's bargain, it's compromise, it's negotiate, it's deal, deal, deal.' In response the mayor Strohn can only offer the politician's clichés of 'law and order' and 'a better place to live'. Ironically he knows less about the system of law and its workings than the dope dealer Leroy whose acceptance into the federal witness programme is being negotiated with Feinstein and Balzic. Leroy's functional black vernacular is admirably geared to the expression of his 'pri-or-it-ies': 'I don't care how long it takes. I do care how soon we begin. And the sooner the better. Like now! We got the righteous shit, man, and we're lookin' to move it. What more you want?'[8]

Just as Balzic acknowledged a necessary relationship with society's marginalised, so Benjamin explored the fringes of the book world in Paris. He not only collected esoteric and disregarded volumes but veered towards the nooks and crannies of those texts. Reading the city, it has been argued, is made simpler by the use of metonymy and synechdoche in order to examine detail and yet bring into focus a broader landscape, Benjamin's chosen example being a crystal from which can be deduced the form of 'the total event'. In his exploration of the city as labyrinth, he preferred fragments to wholes. Determining the larger picture from the fragment in order to illuminate the city's obscurity was the answer to the riddle posed by mystery and intricacy. Since Benjamin, and specifically in the menacing cityscapes of contemporary American novelists such as Auster and Thomas Pynchon, the overwhelming presence of the labyrinth has been the source of paranoia and fatigue: Auster's walker in the city, echoing de Certeau, sees New York as a labyrinth of endless steps.

Historically, the hard-boiled detective novel has been a predominantly urban form in which a challenging milieu tests the protagonist's ability to achieve understanding and mastery. The challenge arises from the size and scale of the city, its power and wealth, and increasingly its ethnic variety. In such narratives, especially from the late 1940s onwards, paranoia has surfaced as a response to the perception of crime as a network of power and control. Thus in a replay of American Puritanism criminality becomes potential in every human exchange. The investigation of the city, conducted textually, becomes a discovery of general corruption and the attribution of blame a metaphor for universal guilt. In contrast to the detective as aesthete (Holmes, Poirot, Wimsey) who remains separate from the environment, the private eye is immersed in events and plays a part in the contingent world of the narrative which writes him as much as, in many instances, he writes it.

The two narratives of detective fiction are the story of the crime made mysterious by the criminal who '*writes* the secret story of his crime into everyday "reality" in such a form that its text is partly hidden, partly distorted and misleading', and the story of the investigation which in the classical model ends with the detective's explanation that closes both stories. In hard-boiled fiction the private eye's enquiries (reading) affects the mystery plot (text) such that it becomes unstable imparting that instability to the PI. On the one hand, he/she uncovers other crimes (blackmail, fraud, bigamy); on the other 'the criminal starts committing follow-up crimes, generally murders, that are intended to keep his story unreadable'. As a result of personal involvement the detective experiences a sense of guilt and moral compromise and is often reduced to 'a paralyzed state of profound weariness and melancholy' like Marlowe at the conclusion of *The Big Sleep*. For this reason and others, the PI is unable to impose justice and restore order. In addition the investigator's exposure of corruption and anti-social practice in the urban milieu effectively removes the power to act. 'The detective's reading venture is thus no longer supported or even legitimized by an interpretive community.'[9]

The detective as narrator is of course the creature of the author, distinct roles separated yet symbiotically linked in Larry Gelbart's award-winning musical *City of Angels* (1992). Set in the California of the 1940s the musical draws upon B-movie and pulp novel conventions to problematise the relationship of human life and its literary counterpart. Stine (literally colourful) is both omnipotent author and defenceless Hollywood hack; his alter ego is the character Stone (introduced in black and white), a private eye, morally stronger and physically harder. Figures in the 'human' narrative have their counterparts in the hard-boiled screenplay, and are soon speaking the lines of movie characters. Stone, disgusted by the compromises being imposed on his story by Hollywood, urges Stine to be a 'tough guy' and takes over the typewriter to rewrite the ending. 'Time I got back to the reality of fiction', concedes Stine.

For de Certeau, making the complex urban maze intelligible invited the panoptic domination of the managed city, the fiction 'that transforms the city's complexity into readability and... freezes its opaque mobility into a crystal-clear text.'[10] For the detective on the other hand, the piecing together of clues and details is an uphill attempt both to create meaning and to map or chart the labyrinth, the mysterious landscape, which is literal and symbolic. The labyrinth though is but one of several major tropes superimposed upon urban centres: in their early formative years Chicago and Los Angeles saw themselves as garden cities. Peter Langer selects four images for the modern city: Bazaar, Jungle, Organism and Machine, of which the first two are of particular interest in connection with the crime novel. They can be augmented by the image of the city as slum.

'Bazaar imagery presents the city in the richness of its activities and opportunities, as well as in its diversity of individuals,'[11] writes Langer, though the notion of Los Angeles as street market in the film *Blade Runner* (1982) is a warning rather than a celebration. The urban labyrinth in this instance is a labyrinth of merchandise. Bazaar, derived from the Persian, evokes the fantasy of the modern city as a place of exotic adventure. In G. K. Chesterton's 'A Defense of Detective Stories' (1901), it glows 'like innumerable goblin eyes' and the glamourous, enticing but enigmatic Orient was a recurrent presence in the classic crime novel from Wilkie Collins's *The Moonstone* (1868) to John Dickson Carr's *The Arabian Nights Murder* (1936). In *Adventure, Mystery, and Romance* (1976), John G. Cawelti claimed that, with the advent of the hard-boiled narrative, brutal reality (corruption, deadly violence) squeezed out 'the Arabian fantasy', though he is obliged to admit it still appears, and could have cited Hammett's *The Maltese Falcon* as evidence. Hammett's insistence on hard facts was self-consciously anti-poetic, but the melancholy of his investigators imparted an element of romance to his city streets.

Sad but enchanted, the cinematic cityscapes of Marcel Carné in the late 1930s serve as examples of rendering the everyday urban scene in a poeticised style drawing on surrealism and silent film. Thus Carné made the city expressive through the shadows of architectural shapes and the symbolism of transport (boats, trains, barges). Carné also used visual images (the sea mist in *Quai Des Brumes*) to enrich the material and the human, part of the process of depicting the city as mysterious, a place where disguise, secrecy and misperception complicate identity and class. It was, though, his associate and scriptwriter Jacques Prévert who brought to Carné's films a fascination with criminals and detective stories.

In American crime movies the elemental struggle between cops and gangsters can assume the dimensions of a war in which men display the ferocity of wild animals. The city as jungle, originally a hobo expression for a dangerous, lawless place on the edge of town, has been one of the most popular images of urban life among sociologists, the ecological dimension offering a way of making some sense (the law of the jungle) of the frenzied struggles of individuals and groups. In addition the dark side of the city was evoked; its spaces were racialised through the white detective who confronts 'blackness' in its various meanings while absorbing mythically romantic aspects such as poverty and marginalisation. The conceptualisation of the jungle also encompassed different predators: ruthless economic competitors and savage criminals who instilled fear and grief. A cultural construct with similar connotations of the unknown and uncontrolled is wilderness, one which associates the PI with his/her frontier origins in the western hero, both mediating between civilisation and contiguous untamed regions.

The perspective of the city as a site of opportunity for the rich and a riot of danger and deprivation for the poor found expression in Upton Sinclair's novel *The Jungle* (1906). Written at a time when Social Darwinism and 'the survival of the fittest' supplied ideological underpinning to *laissez-faire* capitalism, Sinclair's socialist classic exposed corrupt business methods and appalling exploitation of immigrant labour in the meat-packing factories of Chicago, with the city (as jungle) representing in microcosm the larger society of industrial America. The same city provided the backcloth for Bertolt Brecht's exotic fantasy, *In The Jungle of Cities* (1923). During his exile in Los Angeles however, Brecht showed little interest in the city's bohemian margins or its rough working-class honky-tonks and clubs. In *King Kong* (1933) the city (New York) is a primitive urban jungle, but the metaphor enjoyed its greatest Hollywood popularity in the 1950s with John Huston's thriller *The Asphalt Jungle* (1950) and *The Blackboard Jungle* (1955), a melodrama set in an inner city high school where the problems are alienation, delinquency and racism. Although the later film made use of the strident noise of the El train, its studio set of New York failed to convey any sense of place.

While sharing some of the characteristics of the 'jungle' metaphor, the image of the slum focused on a particular location and came to assume certain symbolic and narrative meanings. In the USA the slum, in the sense of streets, alleys and yards where certain conditions of housing and poverty existed, could extend to the size of a district. Urban novelists steered clear of the term and its stigma, but with money and class determining urban residence patterns, it came to represent a strange, mysterious area which the bourgeoisie visited either to dispense charity or for entertainment, hence the verbal form 'slumming'. Trips to Harlem by white New Yorkers in the 1920s fall into this category, with the variation of racial paternalism and stereotyping. Police tactics in the late nineteenth and early twentieth centuries drove prostitution, gambling and illegal liquor sales into the slums so that D. W. Griffith chose to make Hollywood's silent era gangster films in New York's Lower East Side.

Slums, from this point of view, were facts of life, timeless, generalized parts of the landscape like machine shops and forms of rapid transit; poverty was naturalised while being identified in movies of the 1930s as a source of crime. The codes and institutions supported by contemporary ideology remained beyond challenge and analysis. Writers in the 1930s and 1940s demonstrated that the slum was not necessarily a barrier to social mobility; in James T. Farrell's career, for example, success was the consequence of escaping from the inner city slum. However the seeping blandness of postwar suburban life would encourage a nostalgic image of the old slum as an area where hope and pride endured.

In its successor, transformed by *de facto* racial segregation into 'the ghetto', those values would be displaced by nihilism and despair. Increasingly from the 1960s onward the slum turned into a region of empty tracts, smouldering fires and disused buildings, the dumping ground for the detritus of the new, technological 'civilisation'. Hard drugs replaced booze; armed gangs roamed the streets; violent, random crime was endemic. Apocalyptic visions of Europe's cities as magnificent ruins were already familiar in the nineteenth century; by the late twentieth century the demolished city as hell had become a fixture in hard-boiled crime fiction and thrillers, as well as their cinematic equivalents. A trip through the housing projects of Greater Los Angeles by Sue Grafton's detective Kinsey Millhone, prompts this observation: 'The poor sections of every city I've seen have the following elements in common: sagging porches, flaking paint, grass that's tenacious if it grows at all, vacant lots filled with rubble, Pepsi-Cola signs, idle children, cars with flat tires permanently parked at the curb, abandoned houses, lethargic men whose eyes turn vacuously as you pass'.[12]

Sociologists have traced and analysed this lengthy decline – in 1962 Herbert Gans could still entitle a study of Italian-Americans *The Urban Villagers* – pointing to the breaking of neighbourhood ties and the collapse of the family in the face of commercialism and the mass media. More recently Peter Langer has rejected the city-of-strangers scenario in favour of a description of small, local neighbourhoods where history and customs continue to provide control and a sense of identity. In such a mosaic of contiguous and imbricated social worlds, proper names (de Certeau's 'local authorities') would be functionally liberating.

However the perspective of the sociologist is often at odds with that of the urban geographer. Vidler emphasises the deadness, the lack of surprise in the postmodern physical environment: ' suburb, strip and urban center have merged indistinguishably into a series of states of mind ...' and refers to 'already vanished thresholds that leave only traces of their former status as places'.[13] Vidler's only positive suggestion in these circumstances is the emancipating movement of the body across boundaries, seeking its own freedom. The key words are 'loss' and 'dislocation' though not used negatively; the body's action is encouraged by an invasive 'vagabond' architecture, crossing lines and denying notions of appropriateness. The wayward figure of the vagabond (without family, regular work or fixed abode) recalls the traditional private eye (Marlowe, who has but a coat, a hat and a gun). It also evokes the protagonist Quinn in *City of Glass* whose narrative trajectory is from writer to detective to bum, living in a trashcan, symbolically enacting 'a continual movement in the "City of Glass" from the commodity to those forms of rubbish and waste which proliferate in the physical landscapes of a "throw-away" society of instant obsolescence'.[14] More importantly, the action of the body in embracing marginality rejects the entropic obsession in the USA with family values in favour of the adult condition of homelessness, which is accompanied by feelings of loss and demands a confrontation with the uncanny. In the city, security is only precariously sustained by the PI tracking clues through the confusion of modern life. As Baudelaire claimed, the secrets of the city could not be unlocked without knowledge, especially of human nature. The uncanny (in Freud's sense) describes 'something one does not know one's way about in' such as the labyrinthine spaces of the metropolis, where it rapidly becomes associated with criminality, pathology, and that other labyrinth the psyche. The contemporary thriller and film have paraded the greatest number of psychotic killers since the Nuremburg Trials.

NOTES

1 M. Berman, *All That Is Solid Melts Into Air: The Experience Of Modernity* (London, Verso, 1983), p. 165.

2 R. Shields, 'Fancy footwork ; Walter Benjamin's notes on *flânerie'*, in K. Tester (ed.), *The Flâneur* (London, New York, Routledge, 1994), pp. 67, 63.

3 M. de Certeau,'Practices of Space' in M. Blonsky (ed.), *On Signs* (Oxford, Blackwell, 1985), p. 128.

4 L. D. Estleman, *Sweet Women Lie* (New York, Fawcett Crest, 1992), pp. 134, 97–98.

5 C. Prendergast, *Paris and the Nineteenth Century* (Oxford, UK, Cambs., Mass., Blackwell, 1992), pp. 11, 15.

6 Berman, *All That Is Solid*, p. 289.

7 S. Schulman, *Girls, Visions and Everything* (Seattle, The Seal Press, 1986), p. 178.

8 K. C. Constantine, *Always a Body to Trade* (London, Allison and Busby, 1986), pp. 197, 188.

9 P. Hühn, 'The Detective as Reader: Narrativity and Reading Concepts in Detective Fiction', *Modern Fiction Studies*, 33:3 (Autumn 1987), 461, 462. For Marlowe, see Raymond Chandler, *The Big Sleep* (Harmondsworth, Penguin, 1971).

10 de Certeau, 'Practices of Space', p. 124.

11 P. Langer, 'Four Images of Organized Diversity': Bazaar, Jungle, Organism and Machine' in L. Rodwin and R. M. Hollister (eds.) *Cities*

of the Mind : Images and Themes in the Social Sciences (New York and London, Plenum Press, 1984), p. 102.

12   S. Grafton, *'H' is for Homicide* (London, Pan/Macmillan, 1992), p. 132.

13   A. Vidler, *The Architectural Uncanny* (Cambridge, Mass., MIT Press, 1992), p. 185.

14   B. Jarvis, 'Crime in the "City of Glass": The Case for a Postmodern Detective Story', *Over Here*, 10:2 (Winter, 1990), 43.

2

LOS ANGELES

Urban configurations can be distinguished by use of the terms 'capital', implying history, traditions and a politico-cultural centre, and 'metropolis', a network of circulations characterised by a mixture of inhabitants and an amorphous, exiguous identity. While the former has been represented in microcosm by the street, the 'metropolitan' symbol is the freeway, regarded as the agent of liberty and mobility, not least in LA where it has also provided local landmarks and inspired superior public architecture. In Pynchon's novel *The Crying of Lot 49* (1966) however, the invention of San Narciso near Los Angeles as a cryptic text or semiotic system that withholds the full release of its meaning, produces the symbol not of the freeway but of a printed circuit, 'a transference of energy into an endless stream of images and of signs seeking to communicate'.[1]

Sharon Zukin's historicising of Los Angeles as landscape and urban geography in *Landscapes of Power: From Detroit to Disney World* (1991) pinpoints the second, post-1940 LA with its military–industrial activities and its newly unionized labour force as the foundation, through freeways, affluence and suburbanisation, for the apparent realisation of the American dream. Despite the absence of a large manufacturing base, the city would continue to prosper in the years following World War II through foreign investment in banking and a variety of 'high-tech' industries, notably aerospace and software. By the 1970s its dingy downtown was in a state of melancholy decline. In the following decade however, Asian, especially Japanese, and East Coast money poured into the city. The visible expression of those developments in LA (Mark Three) was a glitzy, coherent, New York-style cityscape, Manhattan's excessive building of high-rise office monuments in the 1980s having set the agenda for other American cities.

The appearance of downtown skyscrapers was ironic since one of the major complaints levelled at Los Angeles by European exiles, half a century before, was that in attempting to achieve a 'civilised urbanity' it merely produced inauthentic Parisian or Viennese copies. James Ellroy's fictional panorama of LA in the 1950s was entitled *The Big Nowhere* (1988) and one of the most common indictments of the city it makes focuses on its lack of a centre – its facelessness; the sophisticated would lose their sense of identity as the borders between city and freeway became invisible. Anton Wagner, a German who mapped the Los Angeles Basin in the 1930s used the comparison of cities where the casual observation of street life was a daily practice (especially Paris) to make his complaint about Hollywood: 'In spite of the artists, writers and aspiring film stars, the sensibility of a real Montmartre, Soho, or even Greenwich Village, cannot be felt here.'[2] By the middle of the 1980s the spatial void was being used in such works of fiction as Brett Easton Ellis's *Less Than Zero* (1985) to symbolise the moral emptiness of fictional LA characters. Bored and self-indulgent, they seek to fill the absence with commodities and brand names.

Artists and writers in Los Angeles have served not 'culture' but the Culture Industry. Initially, the role of the city (in Zukin's first version of modern LA) was as capital of the film world and its image factory, making it an emblem not only of the entertainment business, but of commerce and capitalism. Intellectuals from the East who came to work on the West Coast were swift to express their contempt and yet became willing collaborators in the construction of Los Angeles as a type of anti-city.

Its association or confusion with Hollywood inevitably created visual and – through Chandler, Cain and others – literary images of the metropolis. Including within its boundaries Disneyland (at Anaheim), Los Angeles was considered the most mediated place in the USA, and contemporary LA, with its eclectic cityscapes, shopping malls and global village cultures, has been described as a Disneyland lifespace. From the early years of the century when it functioned as the setting for Western movies and therefore as theatrical fantasy space, the visual appropriation of the city has regularly mingled reality and illusion. With its sunshine, beaches, ubiquitous orange groves, and fields of wild flowers a short distance from the financial core downtown, Los Angeles in the 1920s was perceived as a frontier utopia, promising affluence, mobility and a new beginning.

The implication of a paradise is appropriate, the city seeking to represent itself in religious terms. For Eastern gurus, Ojai just outside LA is one of the earth's holy spots and the city has acted as a centre of religious pluralism, the Mecca for a miscellaneous assortment of messiahs, saints and seers whose new creeds and philosophies have often been predicated on science or pseudo-science, conjoining physics and metaphysics. Among such movements are theosophy and scientology, the latter connected through John Parsons to the Satanist, Aleister Crowley. The roster of charismatic individuals includes Aimee Semple McPherson who set up her Angelus temple in Echo Park which she called heaven on earth, and the notorious 'Agent of Satan' Charles Manson. Although the first idealistic colonists of Llano del Rio just outside LA were Young Socialists, successive visionaries with their healing and 'recovery' groups have advocated individual change. The Californian fashion for such groups, especially for Eastern ideas and sages, has often attracted the weak and naive while stimulating the fraudulent and avaricious, a scenario sometimes incorporated within the crime narrative.

The city has persistently been both an observed and imagined environment. An LA discourse can be assembled from signs and concepts: cars, Disney, weather, affluence and catastrophe. Anxious instability has always been characteristic of a city vulnerable to devastating fires spread by the fearsome Santa Ana winds and funnelled down the canyons. Other forces of nature provide comparable threats in the form of earthquakes, drought and mudslides: the writer Joan Didion recalls a childhood divided between summers of dry wells and winters of subtropical rains. At the end of John Gregory Dunne's *True Confessions* (1977) a sandstorm starts to build up in the desert, an appropriate emblem of chance and uncertainty in a novel where the purposeless, disorganized landscape of a diseased, rotting slum is a better ontological guide to the city than LA's structure of business, church, politics and police. The latter confronts the detective Tom Spellacy as a maze while he attempts to establish meanings. The solution to the murder of the 'Virgin Tramp' arrives accidentally with Spellacy obliged to employ the same kind of irrational logic used to decipher his wife's crazy ramblings.

In the 1930s writers of hard-boiled novels, especially Chandler, Cain and their Hollywood counterparts the creators of *film noir*, constructed a sinister, malignant image of Los Angeles, exploding the myth of the city as a golden nirvana gracing the California coast. More recently that negative image has been refined; the ulcerous racial conditions of the city have been publicised by riots and warfare between teenage gangs. From Tod Hackett's painting 'The Burning of Los Angeles' in Nathanael West's novel *The Day of the Locust* to scenarios of urban chaos like *Blade Runner*, Los Angeles with its premonitory smog and heat haze sky has been perceived as a disaster waiting to happen. Its fears, intensified by the promise of pleasure, find expression in appropriate movies, rock songs and books, the danger of apocalypse instilling a sense of entrapment.

Without a skyline (until recently) and despite its identification with Hollywood, Los Angeles has resisted interpretation through a single image such as the skyscraper (New York, Chicago) or the French Quarter (New Orleans). Moreover, LA's fragmentation has produced a city of strangers, where the claims of the community are acknowledged less strongly than in cities with substantial links to the past. Globally, urban work and leisure activities have been bracketed within separate spaces but 'in no other major American city do residents of one neighbourhood read different [newspaper] stories than their fellow citizens a couple of zip codes over'.[3]

For the individual, identity is bestowed as much by town or city as by country or nation. In LA that sense is largely derived from the neighbourhood (Westwood, Hollywood, Silver Lake, Echo Park), increasingly cut off from other neighbourhoods by formidable barriers. Inside the sprawl of similar opaque landscapes, which Edward Soja has called 'a semiotic blanket', a fracturing parochialism and mutual ignorance between social groups and races is intensified by fears of crime and violence.

Ignorance of the condition of Hispanic citizens in the city has been strengthened by the increasing tendency of the white Angeleno, terrified by crime statistics, to keep to certain parts of the city and to visit those by car. Set in a fierce Boston blizzard *Waiting For Rachel Wallace* (Robert B. Parker) offers a rare example of the private eye functioning on foot. An earlier example is Paul Cain's tough guy Gerry Kells in *Fast One* (1932), who has come to California from the tensions of New York but plans to return there. Kells's willingness to walk is not only attributable to his East Coast origins. It represents a rejection, an honourable refusal to be part of a comfortable culture of money, beauty – and cars; even that promise of comfort and Western freedom is illusory in a faceless, corporate LA where movie stars and the tropics have been displaced by business deals and apartment blocks.

For Chandler's Marlowe (in *The High Window*) walking indicates poverty and in Pasadena even the mailman can avoid that indignity. De Certeau's exposition of walking in the city is particularly inapplicable to Los Angeles where, for the most part, it is difficult or impractical to walk. David Rieff records that 'There are few experiences more disconcerting than walking along a wide LA street without the reassuring jangle of car keys in your pocket. These streets are largely unshaded, their sidewalks appearing wider because they are so empty.'[4] He compares the experience to being lost in the desert. The opening of *City of Glass* provides a similar image of aimlessness with the difference that Quinn, for whom walking in the city is a favourite occupation, actively seeks that self-effacing, amnesiac condition as though testing de Certeau's aphorism: to walk is to lack a place.

The projection of menace in 'mean streets' and of its registration as threat by the drifting individual was one of Chandler's particular successes. Transferred to *film noir* that emotional material could generate a variety of narratives. In Hawks's movie of *The Big Sleep* the anti-affluence of the novel is displaced by Marlowe's romantic liaison with Vivien Sternwood. In a city full of what Louis Adamic called 'wild and poisonous growths', that romance provides balance and nourishment, as necessary as the stolen pleasure of the interlude with the assistant at the Acme Bookshop. Other writers and directors used the 'noir' background of LA for more radical and subversive analyses. This was signalled by a geographic move from suburban bungalows to what was once the choice residential district of the city: the dingy Victorian sector of Bunker Hill with its tall single-room occupancies where, in Chandler's *The High Window*, 'hagged landladies bicker with shifty tenants'. Now, following the real estate boom of the 1980s, the decrepit rooming houses have been replaced by upmarket apartment blocks, glitzy hotels and the Dorothy Chandler arts complex.

That shabbiness, once the symbol in hard-boiled fiction of moral transgression, appears more communal and humane than the delamination of downtown LA where the surface has been torn off for car parks. Robert Crais' detective, Elvis Cole, in *Stalking the Angel* (1989), still finds dirty streets there, but the Eighties signifiers of men in suits and corporate skyscrapers have turned downtown LA into a 'capital of capital' and a replica of Boston, Chicago or Detroit.

In the heart of that area Frank Gehry's projected Walt Disney Concert Hall on Grand Avenue will be surrounded by the emblems of civic, financial and cultural power; it illustrates the norm of a privatised secure zone whose existence celebrates the success of market values and the abandonment of 'the street' and public space. Gehry's buildings synthesise the spiritual condition of the city: disconnection, anomie, and indifference or hostility to concepts of neighbourhood or civicness. A key work in Gehry's career has been the Frances Goldwyn Library (in Hollywood) where the major considerations – fortification, exclusion and surveillance – encouraged Mike Davis in *City of Quartz* to characterise Gehry as architecture's Dirty Harry.

The bewilderment engendered by LA has been attributed to the combination of horizontality and a conscious rejection of the past. Increasingly that impression demands modification. The heterogeneity of its population challenges the perception that the city is without context or identity. Currently, its Ph.Ds and engineers make it a western version of Boston; its Mexicans, Koreans, Salvadoreans and Pakistanis are creating cities within the city. In Martin Rowson's graphic novel *The Waste Land* (1990) which renders T. S. Eliot's long poem as a hard-boiled narrative, the famous HOLLYWOOD sign becomes HIMAVANT (that is, Himavat or Himalaya), and the final frame of Shanty Town's restaurant and go-go bars includes the Café Tibetisch with notices in different East European and Middle Eastern scripts.

Even the dystopian mappings of Los Angeles, like *Blade Runner*, have conferred a flickering glamour and existential excitement on the city allowing it to fulfil its historic reputation for newness and possibility. *Blade Runner's* predictions of the future city – as a multilingual, turbulent Tower of Babel – are enticing while alarming. A contrasting paradigm of the future presents LA as a dreamscape of freeways, a Miami-like façade of infinite pleasure. Behind that facade lies the economic power of global corporations controlling communications and expression while satisfying consumer desire.

The Los Angeles of the 1980s and 1990s differs radically from Chandler's 'big dry sunny place with ugly homes and no style, but good hearted and peaceful' (*The Little Sister*). Economic growth and diversification have been visibly dramatic: 'the petty hustlers of yesterday now live in General Sternwood's mansion, Chandler's idea of "old" money.' The swimming pools once used as an index of sybaritic corruption are now ubiquitous. Cocaine, sex shows, liposuction, gay pride, and shopping malls have supplanted Chandler's gaudy, vulgar world of neon, sleaze, and greasy spoon drive-ins. The commercialisation of LA's suburbs is predicted by Mildred's three restaurants in James M. Cain's *Mildred Pierce*. With their neon signs and large parking lots they are early examples of the conjunction of business and the roadside which would culminate in McDonald's 'drive-thru' establishments. Moreover contemporary LA's routine violence and relentless greed are extrapolations of the milieu explored by Marlowe (and Cain) with its 'remarkable core of corruption, of promise deliberately or stupidly unfulfilled [and] of naked chicanery thinly veiled'.[5]

In the 1930s the atmosphere of Chandler's city still resembled that of a country town that was rapidly modernizing, enabling Marlowe in *The High Window* to savour the combined smell of dust, sunlight and car exhausts. That nostalgia can, for literary purposes, be turned into something more dyspeptic and crabby; in *The Little Sister* Marlowe, describing a hotel lobby, observed that the evocation of old cigars persisted 'like the dirty gilt on its ceilings'. Nevertheless nostalgia was an intrinsic part of the detective's yearning and desire as he reminisced of a time when Hollywood was simply frame houses and (then as now) trees shaded Wilshire Boulevard.

Nature and climate play crucial roles in the poetic layering of the narratives: Chandler's LA consists of distinctive suburbs and landscapes within which numerous discontinuities emerge: seacoast and desert; plateaux and mountains; tropical plants and oil wells. Chandler as botanist uses vegetation to differentiate parts of the city and to function symbolically. The process is direct in *The Big Sleep*: General Sternwood's forest of orchids with their fleshy leaves and pungent odour ('the rotten sweetness of a prostitute' for Sternwood) is an index of depravity. In *The Little Sister* Chandler juxtaposes the purity of jacaranda trees starting to bloom in Beverly Hills with the violation of 16-year old virgins in local bordellos. His texts are often suffused by representations of weather, the torrid heat of *Farewell, My Lovely*, the inhuman drenching rains of *The Big Sleep*, a novel in which the continuous changes of weather impose coherence and rhythm, and above all the fierce Santa Ana winds of *The High Window* which sear the landscape and drive Angelenos to murder. Leaves and flowers exposed to the hot winds are withered and blackened ('Red Wind').

Reyner Banham insisted that the language of design, architecture and urbanism in LA was the language of movement. Marlowe noted that the freeways were 'loaded with people going places' even at midnight. For his part he does not tap phones or stake out apartments though he shadows suspects in a small Oldsmobile. Tailing Geiger (in *The Big Sleep*) the PI leaves Laurel Canyon Drive to follow his quarry down 'a curving ribbon of wet concrete which was called Laverne Terrace'. Thus Chandler's language has conveyed the movement from the known to the unfamiliar.

Freeways and travel by car are central elements in the fiction of James M. Cain where the road leads not to freedom but to death. From the opening of the film version of *Double Indemnity*, in which Walter Neff hurtles through downtown Los Angeles headed for the office where he will make his dying confession, director Wilder's protagonist is continually driving. The novel gives a tour of LA and Southern California which encompasses Santa Monica on the Pacific Coast, the oilfields of Long Beach, and the Nordlingers' Spanish-style 'House of Death' in Hollywoodland under the famous sign on the hillside. In the movie the tour takes place in a forlorn landscape of dismal apartments, shadowy streets and anonymous office buildings. The Pacific All-Risk insurance company offices (the name is significantly changed from the novel's General Fidelity) strongly resembles a prison. It constitutes Wilder's vision of corporate mass society, uniform and dehumanised, one he would later use more ambitiously in *The Apartment* (1960). At Jerry's Market, a Hollywood grocery, the murderous lovers meet, paradoxically, in the store's cold, empty privacy. Throughout, Neff inhabits public space but remains absent from social space, a measure of the isolation he shares with many of the film's LA locations.

Los Angeles still contains, within the city limits such flora as juniper and night jasmine, in addition to such locales as mountain tops, narrow rural lanes and deserted canyons. It is among the sagebrush of Purissima Canyon that Marlowe is beaten unconscious, waking to discover the body of Lindsay Marriott. Nature cannot escape the insidious taint of urban crime and malice which confronts the protagonist at every turn. Later in the same novel, *Farewell, My Lovely*, Marlowe is taken beyond the vices of Hollywood and past Beverly Hills into the 'still dark foothills' where the cry of the quail is heard. Here too, urban brutality and ruthlessness are housed in Jules Amthor's angular modernistic building. In the novels of Joseph Hansen, on the other hand, life in the city, where cosmopolitan values and civilised pleasures are preponderant, is endangered by rural primitivism including religious fundamentalism.

The threat of violence in *Skinflick* (1979) and *Gravedigger* (1982), is located in settings beyond the metropolis, such as mountains and desert. Hansen's claims investigator hero, Dave Brandstetter, is homosexual so that in celebrating Los Angeles the author is celebrating sexual diversity and tolerance.

For critic Fredric Jameson the white fence/barrier at Purissima Canyon marks the end of space, an image mirrored later in the text by the gambling boats which, moored beyond the three-mile limit, invite the imagination to dwell upon the vastness of the ocean.[6] Ironically at the end of *Fast One* Kells's career and life are terminated through the semiotic combination of bad weather, the California coastline and his particular *bête noire*: the car. Here also the end of space is registered, signified by the confluence of cliff road and the Pacific, with the protagonist craving the night and the darkness. In Cain's *Mildred Pierce* a crucial scene is composed of similar materials. Trapped by a flash flood Mildred leaves her car to battle her way home through a dreadful storm. The incident takes place between the geographical co-ordinates which represent: her single-minded desire for affluence and social success – Glendale with its typical red-roofed, white-walled tract home – and exclusive Pasadena, its mansions built by old money.

The Lady in the Lake is set in small town California close to the Sierra Madre mountains. Little Fawn Lake is 'like a drop of dew caught in a curled leaf' yet both landscape and suburban society are vulnerable to individual acts of evil. The image of Crystal Kingsley's body floating in the lake represents an incongruity staining nature itself, and the discovery, next to a little pier left behind by a Hollywood crew, draws textually on the Gothic language of freaks and nightmares. Chandler's disciple Ross Macdonald would include a similar scene of disturbance within nature – the discovery of a body in a forest fire – in the ecological crime novel *The Underground Man* (1971).

The town/country contrast (Bay City/Fawn Lake) extends to the representatives of the law: Sherriff Jim Patton is identified with homesteaders and the frontier past. While this underlines the book's melodramatic fixity, the abandonment of moral relativism is again concealed by duplicity. Chandler's lethal blonde, Muriel Chess, dresses in black and white. The paradisal elements of Fawn Lake (tame deer cross the street in Puma Point) are compromised by the tourist invasion characterised as neon, motor horns, cigarette smoke and 'the blur of alcoholic voices'. Technology is perceived as anti-human and inimical to the natural world; ironically the sound of a plane over the hills beyond the canyon is like a hornet's drone. In addition Jameson's postulate of the 'office' as a figurative category, an empty but instrumental space for those in flight, links the cabin at Fawn Lake with the expensive private homes found in the city.

The paradigm for this metaphor is Marlowe's own office, the detective's workplace, but a space replicated in his various unadorned 'dwellings'. Thus his removal to a private house in *The Long Goodbye* is a crucial development full of implications for Marlowe's career. Finally it should be noted that Jameson's semiotics of the office, the antithesis of dwelling, can be seen as a variation of Vidler's 'homelessness'. Fleeing from family values the human body accepts that loss, circulating freely in spaces that permit withdrawal and retreat, spaces where crime or, in the case of Marlowe, the investigation of crime constitutes the work of the moment.

The Marlowe novels are an organised mapping of Los Angeles, 'from the great mansions to the junk-filled rooms on Bunker Hill or West 54th Place'.[7] Earlier, in the nineteenth century, George Lippard, author of *The Quaker City* (1844–5), had made the secluded house Monk-Hall with its corridors and dungeons a Gothic representation of Philadelphia, an autonomous condensation of the city's socio-economic and sexual relations. Chandler 'makes strange' his fictional private dwellings in order to invest material luxury with moral iniquity. The Sternwood house in *The Big Sleep* is a kind of incongruous collage of stained glass, French doors, Turkish rugs and rats behind the wainscoting.

Elsewhere the description of the visually anomalous is a premonition of disaster: the houses of the rich and powerful at Montemar Vista are 'hanging by their teeth and eyebrows to a spur of mountain and looking as if a good sneeze would drop them down among the box lunches on the beach'.[8] The symbolism is as clear as the verbal image of the chaotic murder house in *The Lady in the Lake*, built downwards 'with the front door a little below street level, the patio on the roof, the bedroom in the basement, and a garage like the corner pocket of a pool table'.[9] This surreal construction which qualifies as architecture of the uncanny is not an isolated example within the canon of hard-boiled fiction. In *Double Indemnity*, the garage of the 'House of Death' is under the dwelling, most of which is 'spilled up the hill' in improvised fashion. Generally however, Cain sought to emphasise the typicality of

Californian tract housing in Los Angeles: white stucco houses with red tiles.

Chandler's public places are impersonal and seedy. In rundown hotels with fancy names like *Sans Souci*, a narrow hallway can lead to a lobby where the plants are tired, the sofa cheap and the curtains dirty. The register is signed by Smith, Jones, Smith. ... Commercial buildings have shabby interiors and their anonymous tenants include shyster lawyers, quack doctors and other charlatans. (In a state obsessed with health, several of Chandler's villains are fake physicians.)

Such buildings have their formal, less squalid counterparts in the offices, hotels and apartments of Edward Hopper's paintings. Hopper is generally regarded as the melancholy poet of the modern, alienating metropolis, but his relevance is more specific. As Peter Conrad argues in *The Art of the City* (1984), Hopper's New York is 'less a place than an idea', so that unnecessary details are pared away in a move towards the diagrammatic and abstract. Several paintings depict the theatre: some of his urban types seem to be looking for their roles and identities. 'New York Movie' (1939) is however, more indicative of the artist's enthusiasm.

Hopper was an inveterate even indiscriminate cinemagoer. His ambiguous, night-time evocations of the city and its people in 'Office at Night' (1940), the celebrated 'Nighthawks' (1942), and 'Night Shadows' (1921) establish his connection to *film noir* and thus to Los Angeles. The last-named work, an etching, would serve through its chiaroscuro and its diminished, isolated human figure to epitomise the genre. Hopper's austere environments, often resembling film sets, convey a strong sense of place and, by means of cinematic angles, hint at narrative meaning.

Conrad, in claiming that Hopper's characters have no stories to tell about themselves, accepts too readily the painter's refusal of anecdotal implications. With its high angle perspective and its two characters, a voluptuous secretary and her boss engrossed in troubled thought, 'Office at Night', a picture Hopper liked to call 'Confidentially Yours', bristles with sexual tension. Hopper's procedure is that of the *flâneur*/voyeur, recording glimpses of windows, rooms and people seen on walks or trips on the El train. The results – images of individuals looking or being looked at – call to mind the spying camerawork in the movies of Lang and in Hitchcock's *Rear Window*.

Of equal importance is the question raised of the intelligibility of the city for both spectator and object of the gaze. Hopper's scenes are 'realistic' but more disconcerting than reality. What is the meaning of the spatial relationship of the enigmatic characters, grouped yet separated in 'Nighthawks'? What is the immediate history of the isolated young woman in 'Automat' (1927)? These are the kinds of questions a detective might ask of urban creatures only superficially exposed by the artificial light of American diners.

Architecture in a city of artifice is often a contrived façade in the mechanised technological style of streamlining, or the earlier Art Deco, still found in Bunker Hill cinemas. Chandler's descriptions of modernist design suggest fascination rather than revulsion. He is drawn to the deceptions of Art Deco, to the steps and islands of glass in a perfume company, the Aztec and Egyptian patterns on the monolithic Sunset Tower and the magical exterior of green-tinged Bullock's department store, picked out by violet light. It is that combination of agreeable, exaggerated decoration and neon that transforms LA, often perceived at night and from a distance, into a gaudy illuminated hallucination, a dream world made up of the lights that stretch from Hollywood Hills to the desert. Seen thus it can take on some of the non-human, anarchic force of Joseph Stella's Coney Island lights in his 1913 painting. Towards the end of *Farewell, My Lovely*, even Bay City with its bingo parlours and hot dog stands on the waterfront appears from the ocean like 'a jewelled bracelet' that fades into a soft orange glow.

In *The Lady in the Lake* Chandler challenges the local view of Bay City as a 'very nice place'. Reporting from its 'very nice jail', he calls attention to 'the Mexican and Negro slums stretched out on the dismal flats south of the old interurban tracks'.[10] Realism provides the motivation here for descriptions which fail to form part of a radical response to minority experience: the text proceeds to evoke waterfront dives, marijuana joints, pickpockets, con men and grifters. The impoverished underbelly of the city, or small town, is perceived in terms of criminality.

Race Williams, the first detective to feature in *Black Mask* magazine was a nativist scourge of foreigners and made his initial appearance in the special Ku Klux Klan issue of 1923. Similarly Philip Marlowe's fastidiousness manifested itself in homophobia and misogyny as well as dislike of non-Anglo-Saxon ethnic characters. His attitude towards 'greasers' was congruent with that of LA's white society which pushed the city's large Mexican population east across the river into Boyle Heights and Watts. Walter Mosley, the most praised of the new generation of crime writers, has been compared with Chandler. The two writers share certain LA locations that recur in hard-boiled fiction: corporate offices, canyon roads, Hollywood Hills. However the radical difference in provenance – public school Englishman; African-American and Jewish Los Angeleno – makes the comparison problematic.

A more useful comparison is with the black naturalistic writer Chester Himes, whose LA novels *Lonely Crusade* (1947) and *If He Hollers Let Him Go* (1945), resemble hard-boiled fiction in their racially charged deconstruction of Californian optimism and their evocation of an atmosphere of nervous tension. By setting his novels in the postwar period, Mosley inevitably pays homage to Himes, whom he describes as angry and 'very disenfranchised'. His own black hero Easy Rawlins, though steeled against racist taunts, seeks to avoid confrontation, and when he fails to do so he experiences the frustration and rage which erupt in Himes's Harlem. In *White Butterfly* (1992) he reveals that even in his dreams he feels persecuted by racism. Working on the borders of respectable society he needs to protect the stability and security that ought to accompany property and domesticity.

Rawlins's marginalisation has its costs: the detective fits neither into his own urban community, where his questions arouse distrust, or the official postwar world of the 'Organisation Man'. Ironically he finds himself taking on the monoliths of government surveillance in *A Red Death* (1991): the IRS and the FBI. Constantly engaged like his fellow Afro-Americans in acts of survival, Rawlins cultivates and is embroiled in secrecy: his has been 'a life of hiding'. His inability to communicate contributes to the failure of his marriage in *White Butterfly*. Through Rawlins who cannot explain his brooding existential silence, Mosley expresses a black male anxiety about openness and intimacy.

However, as 'a confidential agent who represented people when the law broke down',[11] Easy Rawlins benefits from his ethnic status when he operates in the shadowy ghetto. To blacks he is, in his own words, 'just another nigger'; to whites he is a version of Ralph Ellison's 'Invisible Man' so that in *Devil in a Blue Dress* (1990) Todd Carter is willing to confide in the black PI: as a rich white man Carter cannot even consider Rawlins in human terms. College educated, Rawlins uses 'black English' to keep him in touch with street life while reassuringly satisfying the stereotypes held by whites. The same imperatives govern his social image: the owner of several buidings as well as the small house on 116th Street, he poses as a janitor calmly sweeping balconies. Using 'white' language is as dangerous as owning a house; both actions suggest an ambition and willingness to transgress the codes imposed by the dominant society.

Mosley's novels constitute a rich portrait of midcentury black life in the immediate postwar period up to the Korean War and the beginnings of McCarthyism. They contain the standard elements of dubious women, homicidal patriarchs and brutal cops. The canyon roads and corporate offices described by Chandler recur but Wilshire Boulevard and Sixth Street are displaced by Avalon, Florence and Central. These are important streets in Watts whose working class inhabitants, shooting dice and drinking from paper bags as they await the occasional labouring job, reveal themselves as transplanted Southerners. The depiction of a black community where an Afro-American identity can be expressed, demonstrates an important shift of perspective; in the Chandler texts it was merely an exotic land of difference into which the white detective had wandered.

Central Avenue had been – in the 1940s – a centre of black power and culture, the focal point for a remarkable explosion of blues, R and B, and jazz, featuring black musicians from Texas, Kansas and Oklahoma. (Joe Louis and Ella Fitzgerald had stayed in the Dunbar hotel there when the city was effectively segregated.) The black detective's professional knowledge enables him to distinguish between places where criminals hang out and doctors treat cuts and bullet wounds, and clubs such as 'Pussy's Den' where B-girls cater for love-starved men and women. Similarly in *Devil in a Blue Dress* he can identify Ricardo's Pool Room on Slauson as 'a serious kind of place peopled with jaundice-eyed bad men who smoked and drank heavily while they waited for a crime they could commit.'[12] The text of *White Butterfly* moves Rawlins through Bone Street in whose clubs beautiful women in furs and silks used to trade drinks with their men as they listened to Coltrane, Monk and Holiday.

Bars and clubs in Mosley's texts, as in those of Himes, provide spaces where black patrons can assume a degree of power; this is frequently associated with illegality. The black lawbreaker, like J. T. Saunders in *White Butterfly*, is a symbolic challenge to the status quo. For part of the novel Rawlins's quarry, he remains distant from the PI and the reader, but the jagged, yellow scar at his throat and the fortitude it betokens are impressive. Saunders is murdered in an Oakland nightclub on the orders of the local police. In LA the Central Avenue clubs declined as police clamped down on racial integration, harassing club owners and white women, so that by

1956, the year in which the novel is set, Rawlins can report that the jazz performers have left for Paris or New York, the sidewalks are broken and the postwar promise has evaporated.

The Watts world, the focus in 1966 for novelist Thomas Pynchon's discussion of urban segregation in LA at large, is one of fragile loyalties, brutality and betrayals even in the First African Baptist Church of *A Red Death*. Afro-Americans hurt and deceive each other but Mosley's villains are usually racist whites, members of the bourgeoisie. His powerful portrayal of the oppression, and virtual segregation of black citizens by the white power structure, is juxtaposed with examples of racial harmony. Chaim Wenzler, the communist charity worker and victim of anti-semitism earns the respect of Rawlins, who is godfather to an abused Hispanic child Jesus Peña. By the end of *White Butterfly* the detective has adopted a second abandoned child.

These tentative signs of hope are set in the past and are over-whelmed in the text by the continual presence of public violence and chaos. The marital rape of which Rawlins is guilty is evidence on a private level of the self-destructive, masculinist baggage which threatens any temporary happiness. Thrown into a police cell, he is comforted by meeting a crazy inmate: sane men had put him in jail. At least Rawlins has his house and trees (apple, pomegranate and banana), his refuge from the concrete jungle symbolising the desire for stability that differentiates Rawlins from the loners in earlier crime fiction.

The characteristic LA experience according to the Pop artist Claes Oldenburg is that of sitting in a car and watching letters silhouetted against the sky. One of the most dominant visual icons in the city is the huge HOLLYWOOD sign: nine wooden letters, twelve feet high, on top of Mount Lee. Thomas Sanchez used this public location, Hitchcock-style, for one of the violent climaxes in his novel *The Zoot Suit Murders* (1978) set in 1943 and, for the most part, in the Mexican-American barrio of Los Angeles.

Drawn like Chandler's Marlowe into a menacing California landscape at night, Sanchez' protagonist Oscar Fuss is directed to the sign when he searches for Hollywoodland, the 1920s sub-division above Hollywood Boulevard which provided the British title for the novel and which featured in *Double Indemnity* (see page 24). The original sign (1923) spelt out HOLLYWOODLAND before the LAND segment slipped down the hill in the 1940s. Sanchez implies a contrast between a small real estate development and a potent myth predicated on the film industry, a difference established by an absence. Fuss's guide, a bearded old man in a long robe and thus a representative of the LA which welcomed faith healers, occultists and theosophists, utters a diatribe based on that absence. HOLLYWOOD is both material object and signifier, its functions combined in the old man's anti-materialistic lament: 'it is just decomposing and falling apart, like everything else temporal and carnal glamorized around here. . . . The whole business is ready to topple over any day, surrendering to time and the elements, nature claiming her own.'[13]

Whereas Ed Ruscha's use of a movie-style sunset in his collage *Hollywood Study* (1966) is vibrantly romantic, Sanchez chooses dusk here to establish a melancholy mood, describing the sign as 'the last advertisement for a feeble civilisation'. The white letters are the symbol of lost promise, an obsolete dream, not least for the dispossessed Hispanic teenagers in East LA, distrusted and manipulated by the representatives of white America.

The summer of 1943 witnessed the Zoot Suit riots when American sailors fought with, and sought to humiliate, young Mexican-Americans or 'pachucos'. Alienated, disinherited, 'orphaned' by the dislocations of recruitment and war work, LA's pachucos defiantly announced their difference through bright, baggy zoot suits, at the same time slipping into delinquency and the drug culture.

Through his idealistic but naïve protagonist, Sanchez exposes American racism but dilutes the examination: the plot is a parody of the detective narrative in which Communist and Fascist organisations struggle for control of the barrio, the latter using a utopian, religious cult as a front. Fuss's simplistic liberalism, the love affair with Kathleen, another Anglo, and the hunting down of the drug dealer Chiquito Banana effectively combine to displace the details of Mexican-American life. Ironically, the novel's political resolution – Communists have planned to scapegoat and destroy the Zoots as a means of blocking the Fascist surge – avoids confronting the ideology of racism and discrimination. Fuss's teenage contact, Cruz, briefly articulates the Hispanic sense of oppression. But the choice of Fuss as central character deprives the pachucos of a powerful voice, able to suggest the possibilities and problems of the 1970s as well as those of the past.

Moving the protagonist beyond the barrio, the text uses familiar signs to convey visual experience. En route to Hollywoodland, Fuss passes Aimee Semple McPherson's Angelus Temple and Grauman's

Chinese Theatre. Looking upwards in tourist fashion he registers in turn the gold dome and the green-tiled pagoda roof. Elsewhere Los Angeles is represented, uncharacteristically but authentically, as an industrial city with a 'concrete horizon'. Looking east Fuss observes a tyre factory and, on the flatlands, alongside grey stuccoed tenements, a forest of chimneys spewing black smoke – possibly a reference to steel mills in the wartime boom town of Fontana. Chasing a lead he finds himself in the equally bleak environment of the San Pedro shipyards where dark streets are still permeated by cold grey fog. Suddenly the Victory cargo ships are revealed by the shipyard lights and by showers of welding sparks, 'a mad display of fireworks'.

Artificial light is also a means of decorating the barrio making it into an exotic spectacle that withholds its full meaning from the white investigator. Sanchez records the neon signs like summer lightning on Flores Street, the Zoot Suiters slouched against shop windows, and their female partners in black skirts and sweaters. Nowhere though does the author explain the cultural significance of these Black Widows (and Slick Chicks) who were also involved in drug trafficking and whose arrogant style constituted a gendered challenge to the machismo of the pachucos. Technological advances in the modern city created the potential for large scale catastrophes: massive fires, factory explosions, chemical or nuclear accidents. In *The Killing of the Saints* (1991), by Alex Abella, the intimations of disaster are among those specific to Los Angeles: earthquakes and the Santa Ana wind. These are supplemented by individual crises such as Judge Chambers' heart attack and Charlie Morell's nervous breakdown. The novel's historical significance lies however in its authentic Latino-American voice and its ethnic setting, the Hispanic districts of LA.

For indigenous Americans the city is associated with loss, displacement, denial and the myth of the melting pot as an homogeneous unity of hyphenated American citizens. If displaced power is merely buried, not lost forever, ancestral energies can be conjured to challenge the authority of the colonisers. In the first chapter of Abella's novel Ramón Valdez, a Cuban-American 'marielito' (see ch. 5, p. 76), makes a vague speech demanding equality and dignity after he and his companion have robbed a jewellery store and, in an horrific bloodbath, murdered (or caused to die) everyone else in the shop. The ruthlessness shown by Valdez initiates an intermittent questioning, by the reader, of the nature of his 'challenge'.

The massacre was committed while the Cuban followers of Santería were in a trance-like state possessed by the vengeful warrior god Oggún. Santería is fully defined in the climactic court scene as a combination of West African religion and Catholicism which emerged and was concealed during slavery, and which holds to a set of beliefs and theological principles. Consequently Ramón is found 'not guilty' on every count, including first-degree murder; the decision has a narrative fitness as the defendant is presented throughout as brilliantly masterful, successfully able to make an individual challenge to the American legal system.

The brief final section, conforming to crime novel convention, undermines this characterisation: when Ramón kills again for money and two keys of cocaine, Charlie Morell the PI protagonist exposes him as a common thief, the cheap B-movie hood he imitates when he enters *Schnitzer Jewelers* at the start of the narrative. After the pair have climbed Mount Hollywood (recalling a similar scene in *The Zoot Suit Murders*), Ramón assumes 'the mask of the ancient god' but is disempowered by the vision of Charlie's dead father and dies on the rocks below.

'It's just you and me, like it always was,' announces Ramón before the final struggle on the hill. Once the Hispanic colouring and supernaturalism are removed, the novel becomes an individualistic, competitive action from the Reagan period with Charlie's urban existence monitored not by the FBI of *A Red Death* but by Ramón's own surveillance network. This opposition (both racial and religious, as Charlie is Catholic) is established in the opening prologue when a white Cuban voice lists the achievements of his fellow immigrants in Miami, 'the Jews of Latin America', while badmouthing the marielitos as 'just a bunch of niggers'. Charlie has his own personal agenda: absolution for the death of his father whose gifts of commendation and forgiveness ('Bien hecho, mi hijo. Estás perdonado.') are complemented Hollywood-style by the rising dawn: 'the City of our Lady, the Queen of the Angels ... sat up to greet the new day.'

Foreign investment, global corporations, Disneyfication, drugs, exotic palm tree Mediterraneanism, artificiality, and a persistent, hopeful focus on the future: these are some of the elements which link LA and Miami. 'We turned it [Miami] into the capital of Latin American enterprise, the center of all the movement of business and peoples who want to be free and shop at Burdines and have a nice condo on the beach, or a house in Coral Gables and drive a late-model car.'[14] Such desires nourish crime and violence: *Body Heat* (1982), the re-make of *Double Indemnity* was set in Miami.

NOTES

1   G. Clarke, '"The Great Wrong Place": Los Angeles as Urban Milieu' in Clarke (ed.), *The American City: Literary and Cultural Perspectives* (London, Vision Press, 1988), p. 143.

2   M. Davis, *City of Quartz: Excavating the Future in Los Angeles* (London, Vintage, 1990), p. 50.

3   D. Rieff, *Los Angeles: Capital of the Third World* (London, Phoenix, 1993), p. 137.

4   Rieff, *Los Angeles*, p. 119.

5   C. Sigal,' The lure of the mean streets', *Guardian Review*, 17 June 1988, 25.

6   F. Jameson, 'The Synoptic Chandler', in (ed.), J. Copjec, *Shades of Noir* (London, New York, Verso, 1993), pp. 51–2.

7   Jameson, 'Synoptic Chandler', p. 53.

8   R. Chandler, *Farewell, My Lovely* (Harmondsworth, Penguin, 1975), p. 43.

9   Chandler, *The Lady in the Lake* (Harmondsworth, Penguin,1952), p. 18.

10 Chandler, *Lady in the Lake*, p. 159.

11 W. Mosley, *White Butterfly* (New York, Pocket Books, 1993), pp. 9-10.

12 Mosley, *Devil in a Blue Dress* (London, Serpent's Tail, 1991), p. 129.

13 T. Sanchez, *Hollywoodland* (London, Methuen,1981), p. 157.

14 A. Abella, *The Killing of the Saints* (London, New York, Serpent's Tail, 1992), pp. 306-8, 1.

3

SAN FRANCISCO

'Most things in San Francisco can be bought, or taken', asserts Sam Spade in *The Maltese Falcon*. Like Los Angeles, San Francisco has a history of vice and violence embracing the exploitation of natural resources such as gold and land, which was followed by the retirement of the perpetrators, hoping to conceal their crimes by hiding away in expensive mansions on what is virtually an island. Dashiell Hammett's 'The Gutting of Couffignal' takes place in a community of this kind, located on a quiet and exclusive island in San Pablo Bay, north of San Francisco. Couffignal's exiguous link with the mainland (a wooden bridge) sustains a dream of solitude and immunity. The island, however, is infiltrated by plausible Russian emigrés, merciless in executing their criminal intentions.

In Chapter Two of *The Maltese Falcon* appears the observation, 'San Francisco's night-fog, thin, clammy, and penetrant, blurred the street' which sets the scene for Sam Spade's visit to the spot in Burritt Street where Miles Archer had been murdered. With its mysterious Chinatown, the city, looking across the water to Alcatraz, was turned by Hammett's novels, and more particularly his short stories, into a hard-boiled, fictional counterpart of Los Angeles. Since then, and while retaining its attractive differences, San Francisco has increasingly experienced the ubiquitous problems of urban America – race, poverty, slums, traffic congestion and the decay of its central core.

The metropolis created by Joe Gores in his DKA (Daniel Kearney Associates) novels of the 1970s, PI procedurals like Hammett's Continental Op tales, is described as one in which 'junkie whores in the Tenderloin and fancy lawyers from Nob Hill are tied together in webs of small-city corruption'.[1] Gores himself insists that the tone of hard-boiled fiction is not entirely determined by urban location: *Interface* (1974), using the same geographical sites as the DKA novels, is markedly bleaker as a consequence of its moral relativism and its chilly central figure. Yet, a later crime novel, Julie Smith's *Tourist Trap* (1986), acknowledges minimal improvements in the Tenderloin as low rents attract immigrant Asian families.

It is an area such as the Tenderloin which Thomas Pynchon examines in part of *The Crying of Lot 49*, a text based on the hard-boiled genre. Unlike the paradigmatic model for narrative in which communication leads to resolution, *Lot 49* postulates a civilisation in which communication fails and there is an excess of clues and signs. While the urban scene implies significance, the city, where meanings are overdetermined, is radically handicapped as a signifying system. As a result, those meanings which do emerge come from the quest for and hope of meaning, as in Geoff Dyer's novel *The Search* (1993) where the protagonist reflects that the right path may be a collection of mistakes and detours.

Pynchon's 'detective', suburban housewife Oedipa Maas looks down upon San Francisco from the Bay Bridge. If San Narciso (LA) is viewed as a printed circuit – the reference is at the beginning of the Los Angeles chapter – the circulation of teeming life in San Francisco is represented as the system of the bloodstream. Oedipa, leaving the protection of her car, goes down to the 'infected city'; riding buses and walking, she has to venture under the highways to gain access to the city's poor and dispossessed: 'she prowled among the sunless, concrete underpinnings of the freeway, finding drunks, bums, pedestrians, pederasts, hookers, walking psychotic.'[2] This miscellaneous group of eccentrics and dropouts is Pynchon's version of the vagabonds and other marginal characters featured by Lefebvre and Vidler. The San Francisco underground is similar to the debris-strewn, pauperised LA ghetto of Watts analysed in Pynchon's 1966 *New York Times Magazine* article, and in *Lot 49* it constitutes the only source of resistance and revolutionary change.

In Hammett's *The Dain Curse* it is suggested that the Temple of the Holy Grail cult chose San Francisco because there was less competition than in Los Angeles. San Francisco has persistently defined itself *against* Los Angeles, which from the perspective of the Northern Californian city, is crassly commercial and vulgar, devoted to profit and pleasure, yet with its hundreds of neighbourhoods, somehow dislocated and hallucinatory. Novelist Herbert Gold has pronounced them the id and ego of the state: in contrast to

LA's sprawling rootlessness San Francisco, formed originally on steep, barren hills at the end of a spit of land, is physically a more focused entity, pretty and settled, a garden city where the tides wash pollution out of the bay. Though many-faceted and comprising a range of atmospheres and spaces, it has avoided LA's diffusion of identity. In *October Heat* (1979) Gordon Demarco's San Francisco PI Riley Kovachs describes LA in 1934 as a larger version of Hollywood, tainted by tastelessness and insincerity, and quotes Chandler's blunt phrase,' a neon-lighted slum'. Furthermore, in a hard-boiled novel with an unusually strong political element, San Francisco, where the challenge to the employers by the longshoremen's union generated a general strike in the Bay Area, is preferred to Los Angeles with its national reputation for union busting and, especially in its police force, widespread corruption.

The materialism represented by LA was self-consciously and rhetorically rejected by the Beats and the Hippies, both firmly associated with San Francisco; they were among the 'hordes of lonely crusaders' who would turn the city into 'a Tivoli of small, sweet restaurants, coffee houses, little theaters, poetry readings, neighbourhood art and culture and salvation centers'.[3] Historically, the ambience has encouraged bohemianism based on literary culture, and cosmopolitanism based on the influence of Europe and the Orient leading to comparisons with Naples and Haifa rather than Chicago. Kenneth Rexroth who contributed to that image of San Francisco stressed that it was founded by miners, whores, pirates, Latinos and Asians, and that an anarchist circle flourished there in World War Two.

The city's openness to experience, embracing groups of outsiders, enabled the Castro district in the 1970s to become the politically active centre of the gay community in the USA. The representation of San Francisco as a Mecca for homosexuals occurs decades earlier in Hammett's *The Maltese Falcon*: when the five principals gather in Spade's apartment to await the delivery of the falcon, three – Cairo, Wilmer (the 'gunsel', a homosexual term for a kept boy) and Gutman – have been identified as gay, although if Gutman's 'daughter' is his mistress, the master villain would in that case be bisexual.

Particular parts of the city function symbolically and appear prominently in travelogues and the collective consciousness of tourists: Fisherman's Wharf, the Golden Gate Bridge, Chinatown, steep streets, Alcatraz, and the city's architecture especially its Victorian, gingerbread houses. Julie Smith in *Tourist Trap* (1986) ingeniously maps San Francisco in the perspective of tourism by recounting the murderous outrages committed by a disturbed terrorist seeking to 'close this hellhole down' – a runaway cable car on Nob Hill, a crucifixion timed to coincide with Easter services on Mount Davidson, shellfish poisoning at Pier 39, and a bomb at Union Square's Bonanza Inn.

Smith provides a journalistic report of the economic dimensions of the tourist industry under threat and a conventional confrontation between psychopath and city authorities. Through her narrator, San Francisco lawyer Rebecca Schwartz, the author does differentiate between mini-mall enterprises such as Ghirardelli Square, once a chocolate factory, and Pier 39, a tacky, fast-decaying, commercialised version of a fishing village which Schwartz indicts as 'a municipal scandal'. Recalling urban disaster movies such as *Panic in the Streets* (1950) and *The Towering Inferno* (1974) which were set in San Francisco, and contemporaneous with Carl Hiassen's *Tourist Season* (see page 80), *Tourist Trap* depicts the city as a ghost town in which even its liveliest street Castro is deserted, and tourists huddle nervously in the foyers of the Fairmont Hotel. But the assimilation of the city's 'gay ghetto' in this way projects it as another stop on the tourist itinerary. and fails to register the power of the gay community at political, economic and spatial levels .

As the Great Fire and Earthquake of 1906 demonstrate, the city, structured by change and upheaval, lives close to disaster, another link with Los Angeles. In two of the DKA novels, *Gone, No Forwarding* (1978) and *Dead Skip* (1972), living in San Francisco's East Bay, 'a big sprawl of nothing [with] housewives driving around in shorts and hair curlers, men drinking beer at the drags on Sunday' is compared with life in the LA subdivisions. In the later novel, Gertrude Stein's notorious comment on Oakland, 'There is no there there', is implied. The work of the agency, repossession, necessitates continual journeys through urban streets, but that work is usually dependent , as it would be elsewhere in California, on the automobile. In the company's case records of violaters, the car in question is listed immediately after the miscreant's name, before any personal details; Lewis Ballard, tracking a suspect, finds it exhilarating to drive on Interstate 280, 'a great beautiful sweep of freeway which ran up the spine of the peninsula',[4] and the text opens with a precise description of a company investigator at work – in his car: 'The 1969 Plymouth turned into Seventh Avenue from Fulton, away from Golden Gate Park. It was a quiet residential neighbourhood in San Francisco's Richmond district – white turning black, with a sprinkling of Chinese.'[5]

Gores is particularly observant of the blurring of racial lines as, one by one, disdained groups improve their social status. The office manager at DKA, Kathy Onada, is Japanese-American, and one of several Afro-Americans in *Dead Skip*, Harrington, explains to Ballard his unusual surname : 'We're *black* Irish, cain't you tell?' Hammett too uses characters of mixed race. Notably Lilian Shan, a rich, young, modern Chinese-American in 'Dead Yellow Women' whose American socialisation (education at East Coast universities, prize-winning prowess at tennis) adds to her ambiguity. Positioned from the start as a femme fatale, she has a businesslike manner that is assisted by 'mannish gray clothes' comparable to those worn by Faye Dunaway as Evelyn Mulwray in Polanski's film *Chinatown* (1974), set in LA. Lilian's case will draw the Op into San Francisco's Chinatown, a dangerous web of interconnecting tunnels and a labyrinth of trap doors and cellars where ruthless Chinese henchmen lurk in the gloom.

'Chinatown' is the embodiment through space and place, of racial ideology. Space is classified to create a social, material construction, a representation based on boundaries and territoriality that results in places of residential segregation. Thus an imaginative geography operates to organise social and political practice. 'Dead Yellow Women' draws upon this historic idea of Chinatown as a ghetto of temptation, corruption and fear. 'Because the "Chinese" were inveterate gamblers, "Chinatown" was lawless; as opium addicted, Chinatown was a pestilential den; as evil and inscrutable, Chinatown was a prostitution base where white women were lured as slaves.'[6] Drabness and difference are signalled by residents who scuffle along in ill-fitting American shoes. However, the Op observes that in the gaudy tourist strip of Grant Avenue the thin sound of a Chinese flute is overwhelmed by the 'racket of American jazz orchestras'. He also explains that the Chinese live in cellars because the street floor is given over to business; later, Joe Gores in the text of the fictional *Hammett* (1975) would deny the tourist myth that Chinese cellars stretch down into the bowels of the earth. Missing in Hammett's 'Chinese' tales is the information that between the wars Chinatown, neither a sink of iniquity nor a model community, still lived with the fears created at the start of the century when it was a seven-block ghetto, and to cross the borders defined by Kearney or Broadway was to risk serious physical injury.

Hammett's short stories were published in the racist literary environment of *Black Mask*. The magazine reflected the imaginative geography of western colonialism, disseminated by Protestant missionaries, which stereotyped Asians generally as comical servants, heathen criminals, faceless hordes (the 'yellow peril') or, in the case of women, glamourous, compliant sex objects. Ideology kept alive spatial categories such as 'Chinatown'. As late as the 1970s New York critics complained that characters in Frank Chin's play *Chickencoop Chinaman* did not speak or act 'like Orientals'. The theatrical reference here is particularly appropriate. In his classic study *Orientalism* Edward Said discussing the representative tropes constructed by Western discourse argues, 'These figures are to the actual Orient … as stylized costumes are to characters in a play.'[7]

In 'The House on Turk Street' (1924), Hammett lapses into cliché ('The Chinese are a thorough people …) but subverts stereotyping by making his Chinese criminal Tai Choon anglicised, poised, articulate and intelligent; though the action is self-interested he saves the Op's life. 'The Creeping Siamese' (1926), refers to Asians who have allegedly robbed the owner of a cinema theatre, a charge which, the Op believes, comes from having seen too many movies. While the godfather figure in 'Dead Yellow Women', Chang Li Ching, teasing the Op with exaggerated and formal Eastern politeness, is a parody of Fu Manchu (perhaps flagged by Hammett who makes Lilian Chan the daughter of a Manchu elder).

Chang Li Ching's son, Quong Lin Get, makes an appearance in Gores' *Hammett*, along with a group of aggressive tong members whom the detective uses to intimidate a speak-easy owner. Gores sets most of the novel's actions in spots that had survived since 1928 capitalising on the considerable number of 'old' buildings constructed after the 1906 disasters and still standing in the 1970s. Chinatown with its ancient St Mary's Church, its ornamented import shops and its restaurants such as Yee Chum's (latterly, Yee Jun's) is no exception. The atmosphere of the neighbourhood permeates the second half of the book as the monstrous activities of the 15-year-old ('looks twelve and talks forty') Lillian 'Crystal' Tam are revealed. Seduced as a pre-teenager and turned into a whore, Crystal is opaque, the very opposite of transparent, and a classic, chameleon-like femme fatale 'totally corrupt and endlessly inventive'. Her perverse schoolgirl giggles signify a characterological relationship with more recent monsters such as Elmore Leonard's psychopaths.

The plot of Wim Wenders' film *Hammett* (1982) departs radically from the narrative of Gores' novel but, set largely in an artificial and mysterious Chinatown, it is suffused by the same mythic 'Chinese' discourse. It retains the Crystal figure as erotic female threat who shares with her corruptor, the underground boss Fong, the otherness of Oriental exoticism. The individualist challenge to corrupt local dignitaries, and the theme of Hammett split between detection and authorship are also kept, and the movie, like the original text, is a pastiche of hard-boiled fiction and classic American *film noir*. During the final credits it reprises the players, in monochrome, performing other Hammett-inspired roles. Pictorially it also evokes *Black Mask* illustrations and Hopper's sombre paintings of urban atmospheres. English Eddie Hagdorn and his gunsel resemble Gutman and the punk in *The Maltese Falcon*; Jimmy Ryan is a more ruthless version of the Op; City Hall symbolises graft as well as the Law; the soundtrack includes foghorns, cable cars and seagulls. Despite its studio origins, the film with its shadows and tracking shots realises a labyrinthine, secretive San Francisco which, appropriately for the subject matter, is both 'true' and fictional.

San Francisco with its hills, steep inclines and sudden drops is an appropriate choice for a movie in which vertigo is central. Hitchcock's *Vertigo* (1958) includes vertical plunges by several characters, but much of the film, particularly the first section is horizontal, as Scotty tracks Madeleine by automobile to the places associated with Carlotta Valdes, enclaves of silence and sadness. These locations and the film's camera movements and slow pace combine to create the effect of a dream or Romantic Idyll, a sorrowful ambience evoking Keats, Poe or the Pre-Raphaelites ; the 'suicide' of Madeleine demystifies them as façades, stage sets for the duplicitous labyrinth into which Scotty is lured by the scenarist Estler.

In the fictions they tell each other, Scotty and Madeleine become wanderers, *flâneurs* who reconstruct San Francisco as a visual space affected by time and history. The sites mapped by their trajectories evoke the nineteenth century, but the 'color, excitement, power [and] freedom' which Gavin Estler, Madeleine's paramour and co-plotter, attributes to the city in that period are displaced by a static aestheticism. In addition, the patterns of circles and spirals that their wanderings make suggest the workings of fate and psychology, and become more evident later in the film when the old journeys are repeated.

Illustrating one of Benjamin's concepts, the city is metamorphosed into a series of interiors (the street as dwelling), linked by the image of the legendary Spanish woman from the 'gay old bohemian days' who, apparently, dominates Madeleine's imagination. They form an alternative tourist's version of San Francisco, both commonplace and strange, one which demands temporal as well as spatial adjustment, in particular the recognition of Europe and culture.

The buildings and places associated with Madeleine proclaim the city (and the world) as art. They include the old Valdes home now a hotel, a wooden Victorian mansion on the corner of Eddy and Gough; the neo-classic homage to its French original, the California Palace of the Legion of Honor whose art gallery houses 'Portrait of Carlotta'; and the Mission Dolores (where Carlotta is buried), once an Indian village, its settlement by the Spanish in 1776 marking the incorporation of the area into their Western Empire. In the second part of the film, Scotty will follow Judy Barton, the 'new' Madeleine, to the Empire Hotel. The most important site lies a hundred miles south of the city but, officially fossilised as a museum, it functions as a micro version of old San Francisco: Mission Juan Bautista, the church bordered by hotel, saloon and houses of wood and stone. Also outside the city, the ancient, melancholy forest of sequoia trees, visited by the doomed couple, is a looming symbol of eternity and oblivion. The city buildings are either lifeless monuments or, in various ways, houses of death. Scotty is trapped and blighted by his urban journeys and by the past; a regional past, and also a personal past which he is condemned to repeat by his obsession with Madeleine.

The McKittrick Hotel, originally the house built for Carlotta, was just a few blocks from the apartments on Eddy Street where Hammett lived and wrote for nearly five years. In Kerouac's *On the Road*, Sal Paradise sees the lights begin to sparkle in downtown San Francisco and thinks of Sam Spade, whose lines Hammett, in Wenders' film, occasionally utters. Monroe Street – just a block long – was renamed Dashiell Hammett Street in 1988, an ironic event since there is no evidence that the city in which he resided between 1921 and 1929 meant anything more to Hammett than the setting for more than half his fiction. The setting is most detailed in the short stories where the unnamed operative for the Continental Detective Agency 'goes into every neighbourhood and encounters every level of society, from bankers with wandering daughters in

Pacific Heights mansions to cheap gunmen living in barren rooms in Tenderloin hotels, who do their drinking in North Beach speakeasies'.[8] 'The Big Knockover'(1927), an example of Hammett's parodic excess, sends the Continental Op through most of those neighbourhoods within the confines of a single novella.

It is a cityscape consciously manipulated in *The Maltese Falcon* where every hotel name is fake, every restaurant name authentic. The uncertainty of meaning produced by this technique points to a larger problem in the tales and early novels created by the Op's verbal performances which are usually detached, neutral and minimally interpretive, as befits an anonymous professional in a modern urban organisation. As Sinda Gregory intelligently shows, the very proliferation of details, such as the names of people and places, compounds the dilemma: 'this sheer bulk of facts actually works against our ability to understand and draw conclusions ... We are so overwhelmed by specifics that it is difficult to separate the significant from the trivial or to gain an overview of what is going on.'[9]

Like Chicago in the novels of Theodore Dreiser, San Francisco, 'Personville' in *Red Harvest* and other cities or towns become the miniaturisation of the social and political condition of the USA, the target for Hammett's critique of American capitalist practice. In *Red Harvest*, the Continental Op, hunting in his dream for a woman in a veil, finds himself walking the streets of America, from Gay Street and Mount Royal Avenue in Baltimore to Victoria Street in Jacksonville. If on the one hand fictional San Francisco is an urban fantasy of intrigue and excitement, the city filled with violent yet colourful characters, a city of rumours, lies and appearances which obstruct the probings of the detective-protagonist, it is also illegible within an existential perspective of fragmentation and contingency. The city, like the milieu of *The Maltese Falcon* defies comprehension. On the social and political level, Hammett's pessimism, which regards capitalist democracy and corrupt wealth and power as ubiquitous and permanent, freezes the city (San Francisco, or in *The Glass Key*, an East Coast city) this side of redemption. In a Darwinian universe shape-shiftings and masquerades are as much survival strategies as techniques of predatory acquisition .

Hammett was writing at a period of major growth and change for American cities. A production economy was being replaced by a consumption economy; modernism was challenging religious and social attitudes and, in alliance with new technology, altering human consciousness and psychology. The physical face of the city was being reshaped in, for example, New York where such structures as the Brooklyn Bridge, the Chrysler Building and the Rockefeller Center were planned as 'symbolic expressions of modernity' – to use Marshall Berman's phrase. San Francisco, however, despite the boast of real estate operator Ben Swig after World War II that a new skyline would make the city a second New York, has with varying degrees of success resisted the spread of high rise developments, especially on the northern waterfront (Pier 39 notwithstanding).

San Francisco remains in the hands of the powerful and rich as it did in the era of flappers, jazz, square black cars and bootleggers. Hammett observed a cultural chaos within the pluralistic, populous city where growth, materialism and the confusion of races would contribute to the proliferation of urban problems. As Thomas Hardy observed of modernizing London, the individual is conscious of him(/her) self but nobody is conscious of themselves collectively. In the new cities of the USA, as individuals cut off from their roots attempted to adjust to new spatial arrangements (and lack of space) in the atomised city, many found themselves without a firm sense of community. Figures jostle, settle or move to new spaces. Hammett represents this urban condition as a vast spectrum of lawlessness, extending it from the social to the cosmic. His image of mass society is established by one hundred and fifty felons swarming upon San Francisco's financial district and robbing two major banks in 'The Big Knockover', or the residents of Personville in *Red Harvest*, cheating, embezzling, lying and killing one another. In these instances Hammett deliberately intensifies the climate of city violence, a process which contributes to the creation of the Modernists' 'unreal city' of licence, strange juxtapositions and uncertain identities.

Red Harvest offers the romantic fantasies of crime, action and the marginal, endangered detective. The text appears in its completed form in 1929, however, the year of the Great Crash heralding a decade of economic and social crisis. The city of Personville is run by the robber baron Elihu Willson and his hoodlums as a 'legitimate' crime syndicate. In the 1930s Hollywood movies would represent racketeers as commercial businessmen, a collective image of capitalism but logically extended without checks from government or unions. As Christopher Bentley shows, the state of Hobbesian warfare in 'Poisonville' is not incompatible with successful industry. In addition, 'the gangsters are themselves a manufacturing and service industry, supplying liquor, gambling, and cheap stolen goods to the citizens'.[10]

Hammett also regularly demystifies respectable American society by proposing the world of crime as a mirror image. But in *Red Harvest* (and elsewhere) his gangsters fall out and are vulnerable to the manipulations of the Op who cleanses the city in the process, opening it up like a body 'from Adam's apple to ankles'. While the gangsters function in a predictable way, driving their black limousines as though they were still in Chicago, the Op uses a number of identities, including that of an IWW member. The Op's poses, along with his investigations and shadowings, are part of his effort as a professional to 'stir things up' so that before long the' reality' around him is exposed as 'a construction, a fabrication, a fiction, a faked and alternate reality' like the social fiction of Prohibition itself. 'And the Op's work therefore is to deconstruct, decompose, deplot and defictionalize that "reality" and to construct or reconstruct out of it a true fiction, i.e. an account of what "really' happened.'[11]

Politics too in Hammett's texts implies fictions and systems manipulated for base motives and operated by characters with at best a tenuous hold on ethical values. Nevertheless, *Red Harvest* does qualify as social criticism, with Elihu Willsson, a combination of Rockefeller and Capone, demonstrating the inseparability of politics, business and crime in the modern city. Hammett's populist suspicion of the city and its values provides no political solutions. In his pre-communist phase, Hammett takes up a stance of mordant indignation yet with a nihilistic relish in mutual destruction. His descriptions of the city acknowledge the wealth and luxury in circulation and, like Chandler later in LA, he observes ironically the general shabbiness, physical and moral, which ensues.

In *The Maltese Falcon*, Gutman's civilised exterior is a sham, with his pose of romantic adventurer decorating his ruthless hunt for the bird which symbolises the novel's many deceptions, as well as incorporating the history of capitalism. The removal of its black paint surface reveals not a treasure but a leaden shape; like the characters in the novel the falcon is counterfeit. It arrives by sea, a reminder that San Francisco, located at the head of a natural waterway system, is uniquely a port city with access to the world's sea lanes. In the novel, it acts as a magnet drawing in rootless characters from the decadent Old World to be confronted by America's representative, tough-talking Sam Spade, able, as Hammett insisted, 'to get the best of anybody he comes in contact with'.

On the one hand, ships and the sea are a stimulus to the imagination: Foucault called the ship the heterotopia (a counter-site
within yet detached from its culture) *par excellence*. On the other,
San Francisco has historically had a more definite *working* relationship with the ocean than Los Angeles; the waterfront, where the
movie *Hammett* begins and ends, activated the establishment of
factories, canneries and packing houses – and the building of the first
locomotive in the West. *October Heat* registers the hissing and
clanging of locomotives as they move along the Belt Line Railroad,
transporting freight cars to ocean-going boats. The novel's description of the Embarcadero is humanised by teamsters, longshoremen,
warehousemen and even tourists, but Demarco is careful to adapt his
genre-painting to the populist attitudes of the hard-boiled crime novel.

> There are pool halls, cafeterias, saloons, tattoo parlors, cheap
> hotels and cigar stores where men talk politics, the union, lot-
> tery tickets and the ponies. Behind are the financial districts'
> skyscrapers, topped with flashy electrical signs that lie about
> prosperity. They dwarf the waterfront slum and serve as a
> nasty reminder that wealth has its privileges.[12]

This industrialisation of the dock area led to strikes and labour-
capital violence which, along with Gold's celebration of the diversity in
San Francisco, 'middle-class strivers, union people, dockmen, straight
insurance clerks, Chinese and Japanese immigrants looking to make
out okay, a large black and Chicano population',[13] modify the more
limited 'bohemian' image of the city. Demarco fluctuates in his
approach to the representation of 'everyday folk', Riley Kovach's
perspective varying according to events in the plot and his own
movements. In Chapter 11, he observes the 'spectacle' of Sixth
Street, its piles of mattresses and household goods and sometimes a
cooking fire surrounded by hungry children: 'an urban edition of
those hopeless settlement camps known as Hoovervilles'.[14] Dismal
scenes of this type colour his observations, in Chapter Two, of those
in work as they leave their offices and shops in the city. Huddled in
small groups, they appear exhausted to Kovachs who feels their
blankness and distance. This is T. S. Eliot's sighing crowd, their
eyes fixed on their feet or, in this case, the pavement.

Later however, having been invigorated by the commitment
and passion of the waterfront priest, Father Windy who runs a one-
man social service at a mission just off the Embarcadero, Kovachs
describes his working class neighbours in the streets around Fourth
and Brannan more positively. He records their anxiety and their

struggles to make ends meet, but their presence in the normally empty streets and the use of such words as 'citizens' and 'restlessness' suggests the latent communal strength of labouring people.

The background to the novel is the gubernatorial campaign of progressive candidate Upton Sinclair, socialist turned Democrat and author of the classic *The Jungle*, and the efforts of fascists and Klanners to undermine it. Once more Kovachs, who has worked on the waterfront and on a union drive in Ohio, learns the lesson that those who oppose corporate power and simply 'fight for the little guy' invite suffering and murderous violence. Yet he refuses to succumb to impotent pessimism and although Father Windy's life is sacrificed, his example and that of others like Tom Mooney help Kovachs to look to the future with a measure of hope. His reflections on the case take place in the Arboretum at Golden Gate Park, another of Foucault's heterotopias, the 'smallest parcel' of the world that is also its totality.

NOTES

1   J. Williams, *Into the Badlands* (London, Paladin, 1991), p. 117.

2   T. Pynchon, *The Crying of Lot 49* (New York, Bantam, 1967), p. 96.

3   H. Gold, *A Walk on the West Side: California on the Brink* (New York, Arbor House, 1981), p. 207.

4   J. Gores, *Dead Skip* (New York, Random House, 1972), p. 71.

5   *Ibid.*, pp. 81,1.

6   K. J. Anderson, 'The Idea of Chinatown: The Power of Place and Institutional Practice in the Making of a Racial Category', *Annals of the Association of American Geographers*, 77 (1987), 589.

7   E. Said, *Orientalism* (New York, Pantheon Books, 1978), p. 71.

8   D. Herron, *The Dashiell Hammett Tour* (San Francisco, City Lights, Books , 1991), p. 2.

9   S. Gregory, *Private Investigations: The Novels of Dashiell Hammett* (Carbondale, Southern Illinois U.P., 1985), p. 42.

10 C. Bentley, 'Radical Anger: Dashiell Hammett's *Red Harvest*' in B. Doherty (ed.), *American Crime Fiction : Studies in the Genre* (London, Macmillan, 1988), pp. 64-5.

11 S. Marcus, 'Dashiell Hammett and the Continental Op', *Partisan Review*, xli: 3 (1974), 370.

12 G. Demarco, *October Heat* (London, Pluto Press, 1984), p. 117.

13 Gold, *Walk on the Wild Side*, p. 62.

14 Demarco, *October Heat*, p. 43.

4

NEW YORK

If the discourse of LA (mobility, weather, fantasy) is constituted by conditions, that of New York is derived from people – Whitman, Stieglitz, la Guardia, Rockefeller, Moses, Gambino; places – Coney Island, Harlem, Park Avenue; and architecture – the Brooklyn Bridge, the Chrysler and Empire State Buildings. Legendary names, historic locations and dramatic architecture project a vision of New York in terms of magnitude, variety, energy and power.

By the early twentieth century Manhattan's skyscrapers were already identifiable as notably flamboyant and imaginative, a functional counterpart to the magical domes and towers of Luna Park and Dreamland at Coney Island. This is the proposition of Rem Koolhaas in his landmark book, *Delirious New York* (1979) which identifies congestion and fantasy as the distinguishing features of Manhattan's social and visual culture; one threatened by the International Style with its priorities of rationality and functionality. So the city's image was one of determined theatricality modified by pragmatic business sense. In reality mediocre buildings inspired by speculation sprang up all over Manhattan; the exceptions ransacked the history of architectural styles producing Gothic office buildings and, in the concourse of Penn Station, an imitation of the Roman baths at Caracalla.

The city's ambivalence can be inspected in the contradictory descriptions offered by observers. The photographs of Riis and Hine reveal the dense enclosed spaces of streets and alleys, and Lewis Mumford, like many others including Le Corbusier, deplored the restriction of light and air in the chasm-like avenues. Conversely, he celebrated the intense blue sky of crystal-sharp days in early autumn. While he recoiled from the paralysing noonday clouds of smog, he welcomed the sea fret in spring as an announcement from the ocean.

Sartre also was responsive to New York's sky and weather recording the essence of the city as 'a savage sky above parallel highways', a combination which reached outwards connecting New York to the rest of the USA. The avenues which striped Manhattan gave the island its meaning: far from constraining the environment, they facilitated mobility. 'Our cities in Europe are built as a protection against space; the houses huddle like sheep. But space traverses New York, animates it, stretches it.'[1] Despite the exhilaration afforded by space, Sartre believed that individualism was reduced by the simultaneity of lives and by numerical anonymity. In the opening of *City of Glass*, Auster's central figure Quinn registers a similar experience: disoriented by labyrinthine 'inexhaustible space', he feels lost, both geographically disoriented and personally bereft.

When urban electrification began, American cities were significantly brighter than their European counterparts. The gap was wider at the end of World War II when Sartre and Simone de Beauvoir issued their appreciations. To them New York was a modern version of the Thousand and One Nights, a site of luxury in stark contrast to Europe's devastated cities. At that time city illumination had an ideological dimension. Dorothy Hughes's *The Delicate Ape* (1944) was set in 1956, just before a conference which might sanction German rearmament. The protagonist, equating the lights of Broadway with the lights of the world, pledges to ensure their continuance. The impressions of the French visitors were based on Manhattan Island which despite its danger spots – such as the Port Authority Bus Station and the West Side Highway and its environs – remains the vibrant core of New York. Ironically, parts of the surrounding boroughs with their pot-holed roads, empty decaying factories and rubble-strewn lots are a late twentieth century reminder of those postwar images.

One such area is the notorious Bronx, the scene of hundreds of murders and rapes and around 15,000 robberies each year, most of the perpetrators and victims Afro-Americans and Latinos. It was also one of the settings for Tom Wolfe's 1988 novel *The Bonfire of the Vanities* in which an affluent bond salesman, Sherman McCoy strays from his protected Wall Street/Park Avenue existence into the Bronx and is involved in an accident which leaves a black youth in a coma. These events make him vulnerable to the operations of the criminal justice system and to the activities of lawyers, journalists and black activists, all with their separate agendas.

In his determination to expose the moral emptiness of the Reagan years, Wolfe concentrates on surface appearance, on clothes and physique. The affluent possessions of McCoy, 'the Master of the Universe' and his set are relentlessly listed – his $650 New & Lingwood shoes from Jermyn Street, London, his marble entry gallery and especially, his $48000 Mercedes sports car. McCoy is as car oriented as a resident of Los Angeles. Avoiding the graffitti covered subway which his ex-CEO 71-year-old father continues to patronise, he takes a ten dollar taxi ride to his office and hires a limousine to attend a ritzy party six blocks away. His two cars are expensively garaged in Manhattan.

For McCoy and his set the metropolis is, as Wolfe announces, the destination for those 'who insist on being where things are happening'. To preclude unsettling incidents he follows the advice of a friend who believes the secret of living in New York is to insulate yourself from 'the trenches of urban warfare' by taking cabs around the city. His mental picture of New York is based on Manhattan's roads; when he ends up in the Bronx he has 'lost track of the grid pattern' and, it gradually ensues, lost control of his life. McCoy's perceptions which will result in panic are produced by ignorance – he mistakes a chair stuck in a cyclone fence for a woman's head.

Another fictional character bemused by the lack of a grid pattern is Michael Barnes in Ed McBain's *Downtown* (1989). Like most out-of-towners visiting New York, Barnes, an orange grower from Florida, would normally keep within the confines of the midtown area. The application of concepts of urban spatiality to fiction necessitates the acknowledgement of boundaries as well as psychological relationships to the environment. Barnes's relationship to downtown, the section of Manhattan below 42nd Street, rapidly becomes one marked by disorientation, concern and bewilderment, emotions felt by characters in Dorothy Hughes's novels (for example, *The Fallen Sparrow*, 1942) uncertain whether they are being pursued or simply in fear of their own shadow. Fear would be an inappropriate term in *Downtown* since Barnes, throughout the novel, can respond to dangerous situations by recourse to wisdom acquired in the jungles of Vietnam. By the end of Chapter Two he has been robbed of his money, credit cards and rented car; walking and running at night in an alien city covered by snow at Christmastide intensifies his perplexity.

His situation is ameliorated by the assistance of Connie Kee, a Chinese immigrant who has, to his perception, the 'sinuous glide' of Orientals, but who challenges stereotyping with her height (five feet nine) and her job as a chauffeur. Connie's limousine supplies transport for Barnes's attempts to retrieve his property and track down the criminals. It also provides occasions for Barnes to discover the inadequacies of his efforts to map the city.

The basic premise of the narrative, the wrenching of an individual from his routine and sources of security, suggests the movies of Hitchcock, as well as *film noir*, for which Hughes's novels were an important source; *Downtown* is a book where intertextuality is used to confuse appearances, adding to Barnes's problems in decipherment. A character will be a Marilyn Monroe look-alike 'with a Carly Simon mouth'; another will use 'a dirty Eddie Murphy laugh'. The book's climactic action in the backseat of Connie's limousine is described as 'a good movie' and the cast includes the 'fat motion-picture director' Crandall whose office in the delapidated Bowery Palace Hotel is searched by Barnes and Connie at the start of their hunt.

With its dangling electric wires, its bulging ceiling, collapsing posts, peeling wallpaper and, above all, its well-filled spittoon, the hotel lobby recalls earlier examples in hard-boiled fiction such as the Fulwider Building in Chandler's *The Big Sleep*. McBain however, offers a contemporary trope to separate the overlaid images: his building looked as though it had been 'attacked by terrorists with pipe bombs'.

Barnes's odyssey takes him to Crandall's apartment from where he enters the wilderness of the Lower East Side on a search for St Luke's Place. He becomes 'lost in space' and moves in circles as thoroughfares zig-zag, and numbered streets are displaced by names which are meaningless or deceptive: Broadway in lower Manhattan looks nothing like the Great White Way. Later, in the final chase as place names blur into street names, he has to remind himself: 'Albany on the left, the street, not the city, and Thames on the right, the street, not the river'.[2]

Nevertheless Barnes's adventures move him inexorably towards the Hudson River, and as his mapping of downtown acquires substance he deludes himself that he is beginning to learn the downtown area, encouraged by the recognition that the cityscape with its tall buildings, its movie theatres and restaurants is alluring and literally dazzling especially at Christmas. His quest ends at a discotheque in a section of town where the various textures – the glamour, the disorientation and above all the fantasy – are concentrated.

> Oz was a disco on a peninsula that hugged the exit to the Battery Tunnel. Located on Greenwich Street, as opposed to Greenwich Avenue farther uptown, it seemed undecided as to whether it wished to be closer to Edgar or to Morris, which were streets and not people. In any event the club was so far downtown that in the blink of an eye the West Side could suddenly ... become the *South* Side, for it was here at the lowest tip of the island that West Street looped around Battery Park to become South Street.
>
> 'It's all very confusing,' Connie explained, 'but not as confusing as the borough of Brooklyn.'[3]

Barnes's geographical confusions are aggravated by epistemological ones. Most of the clients at Oz are dressed like characters from The Wizard of Oz. Appropriately it is at Oz that he not only confronts the dedicated killer 'Mama', but discovers the name conceals a Colombian drug dealer, Mario Mateo Rodriguez. In the back seat movie, Mama smiles like one of the bandits in *The Treasure of the Sierra Madre*.

Identity is also at the centre of Sarah Schulman's lesbian detective novels. *The Sophie Horowitz Story* (1984) functions as an example of Bakhtin's masquerade in which identities are destabilised and high figures are humiliated or exposed; in this case the DA is a dealer in stolen goods, winos (who drink only coffee) are undercover agents. In contrast Laura Wolfe the revolutionary (Women against Bad Things) is disguised as a nun. Mrs Noseworthy, a wrinkled, grey-haired old lady and mystery writer in the Miss Marple mould, subverts the stereotype by driving a lavender BMW. Through her and the book's narrator, the feminist journalist Sophie, the fiction of the super-detective relentlessly seeking out truth is undermined. Sophie's fumbling investigation is frequently suspended for the purposes of gratifying activities such as food, clubbing and sex; and her quest for Laura Wolfe, which represents her as slinking around like Sam Spade, is a set-up, controlled and manipulated by the old time radicals. The authorial perspective and the practice of representation have been regarded as antithetical to the spirit of carnival with its focus on the corporeal and cyclical human life. As if in response to this textual dilemma, the characters in *The Sophie Horowitz Story* actively disappear: Sophie herself recedes into city life and her writings for *Feminist News* are thrown away and thus erased.

The Sophie Horowitz Story is in part a celebration of the Lower East Side, with its coke dealers, Polish women at the hairdresser's and Puerto Rican men hanging out listening to Tito Puente, the area remembered sentimentally by Sophie for trips to the Yiddish theatre with her grandmother and kasha varnishkas (dumplings) afterwards at the dairy restaurant. Although the clock at the zoo still plays 'Silver Bells' on November 1st, the neighbourhood is now threatened by the prospect of developers' high rise condos.

Girls, Visions and Everything (1986) is rooted in the same local geography, its street mappings signifying a particular marginalised community of the poor and vulnerable, a variation of the vicious underworld of the masculinist crime novel. The central figure of Schulman's second book, Lila Futuransky offers a female perspective of the city. Yet her isolated situation 'a poor Jewish lesbian, pitted against the burgeoning bourgeoisification and consequential break-down of her urban community'[4] still suggests a link with the classic hard-boiled detective. This work, part social realism, part street poetry, and its successor, a crime novel entitled *After Delores* (1988), are nostalgic for the vibrant downtown space where 'multicultural refugees' support each other and resist gentrification. But Lila's dreams and obligations, her search for self-identity take her down those dangerous streets where anti-woman and anti-homosexual menaces lurk.

In *The Bonfire of the Vanities* Wolfe realistically depicted the bleakness of the Bronx: 'Utterly empty, a vast open terrain … streets and curbing and sidewalks and light poles and nothing else … the hills and dales of the Bronx … reduced to asphalt, concrete and cinders … in a ghastly yellow gloaming.'[5] The same Bronx city-scape visited by Burke at the beginning of Andrew Vachss' *Hard Candy* (1989) is peopled and moralised in the tradition of Chandler's analytical descriptions of public areas: 'Blacked out windows in abandoned buildings – dead eyes in a row of corpses … Whores working naked under clear plastic raincoats stopped the trucks at the lights. We crossed an empty prairie, tiny dots of light glowing where things that had been born human kept fires burning all night long.'[6] Specifically the location is one of the most desperate in the metropolitan region: the heavily fortified Hunts Point meat market and its surrounding junkyards, bars and liquor stores. Elsewhere Vachss provides a symbolic image for 'the prairie': a Darwinian battle between wild dogs and seagulls for slabs of fat.

Vachss' vocabulary in his interview with John Williams in the travel book *Into the Badlands* – 'absolutely the end', 'no-man's land', 'exclusively hardcore' – suggests a level of decay and sociopathic evil which finds its correlative in the crimes Burke specialises in solving: child pornography, and the sexual abuse and murder of children. A retributive avenger, a brave and obsessively moral outlaw who operates, like his adversaries, beyond society's rules, Burke is a mythic, urban comic strip figure whose bailiwick could easily be Gotham City. His office is protected by the electronic surveillance techniques identified in Los Angeles by Mike Davis; his accomplices, marginalised by straight society, include a gigantic, mute Mongolian, a transsexual hooker, and an anti-Nazi genius who lives in the Bronx wastelands with a pack of wild dogs. This cyberpunk family confronts the anarchy of the contemporary city, where 'teenage robot-mutant millionaires' dispute the distribution of cocaine, but fails to ameliorate the characteristic loneliness of the hard-boiled investigator.

The agenda of Wolfe's narrative excludes consideration of those issues crucially affecting the lives of minorities and the marginalised: homelessness, drugs and AIDS. His apprehension of urban deterioration is broadly based and is joined with a naturalistic prose predicated on notions of the human jungle or wilderness.. In the Bronx itself the modern city is erased as officials in the courthouse obliged to work after dusk engage in 'wagon-training', moving their cars in formation to a safer car park. Urban pathology, exaggerated in the Bronx, enfolds McCoy who is traumatised by his arrest, his distress and victimisation by the media registered by Tom Wolfe through animal imagery. The mob of reporters and cameramen is like 'a huge filthy sprawling dog': 'they were the maggots and the flies, and he was the dead beast they had found to crawl over and root into.'[7] A naturalistic discourse of decay contributes to the novel's vision of urban breakdown in the Reagan era of greed and moral degeneration. Despite the book's length and panoramic surface, Wolfe's representation of the city is limited by blunt realism, the indiscriminate nature of its satire, and a lack of insight into the lives of black citizens and women in New York.

The expensive lifestyle of a Sherman McCoy (or a Donald Trump) is the defining characteristic of several earlier New York detectives or surrogates of whom Nero Wolfe is the most renowned. The creation of Rex Stout in the 1930s, Wolfe, a rich, grossly

overweight, consultant detective who takes little exercise, lives in
an old brownstone house on 35th Street, which he rarely leaves.
The moral opprobrium attached to wealth by Chandler and others is
removed: like General Sternwood, Nero Wolfe is associated with
rare orchids, but unlike the General, has a lifestyle of sheer pleasure
and self-indulgence: black silk sheets, a private elevator, a personal
chef who creates Duck Mondor or Petit Saucisson. Stout's only con-
cession to proletarian taste in his protagonist is the chilled beer
which Wolfe drinks at the cocktail hour.

The necessary exploration of New York is carried out by his
secretary Archie Goodwin or by the PI and disguise expert Saul
Panzer. Hammett's *The Thin Man* (1932) in which whiskey-
swilling, partygoing Nick Charles 'investigates' murder in a laid
back, indolent manner, is set in New York, and demonstrates the
ability of the professional to use the city, probing it as part of the
crime solving process. Although distanced by residence in a hotel,
Nick and his wife Nora use the city's technology – telephones, taxis
– to function and make connections.

Reuben Frost's brownstone house, in novels by Haughton
Murphy, is on East 70th Street and while, like Nero Wolfe he
represents a refined New York society now disappearing, he is less
sybaritic and rarefied. A retired Wall Street lawyer, he shares
Mc.Coy Senior's preference for the subway when he is not taking
Avenue buses or, despite being mugged in the street, simply walking.

De Certeau, in 'Walking in the City' makes a distinction between
voyeurs and walkers. The former crave a god-like totalising gaze
with which to view and read a panoramic picture of the city. The
ordinary practitioners of the city, in contrast, 'follow the thicks and
thins of an urban "text" they write without being able to read it'.
The urban and spatial practices involved refer to a characteristic
'opaque and blind mobility'.[8] In *City of Glass* Quinn endeavours to
transcend the limitations of the walker, to become an all-seeing
voyeur (*City of Glass* tropes on the title of St Augustine's *City of
God*) – by obsessive walking! He likes to wander wherever his legs
take him and whatever the weather in order to cultivate that
'opaque and blind mobility'. It is on his *best* walks that he feels he is
nowhere. As a writer of mystery novels who plays detective, he
interprets the term 'private eye' as investigator, as I, the self, and as
the observer's seeing eye, 'the eye of the man who ... demands that
the world reveal itself to him'. By emphasizing the importance of
signifying language (and therefore of signifieds), the author draws

us into the detective's project with its promise of a solution: 'no circumference can be drawn until the book has come to its end.'[9]

Despite the presence of genre figures – the loyal retainer, the seductive *femme fatale* – the circumference remains undrawn. The narrator subverts, deconstructs the linear quest of the detective and substitutes the postmodern experience of endless loopings with no apparent destination, or locus of truth and meaning. Brian Jarvis summarises the novel as 'a labyrinthine textual maze of interpretive "cul-de-sacs", treacherous darkened alleys which are a formal reduplication of its subject's experience of the city.'[10]

This is in line with de Certeau's description of an urban surface order ruptured by ellipses, drifts, and leaks of meaning. In the narrative de Certeau's 'graphic trail' is represented by the spatial journeyings of Quinn. He maps the footsteps of his quarry Stillman (Senior) in his notebook and arrives at the message: THE TOWER OF BABEL. The heterogeneous chaos this implies is found less in the landscape than in the ragged drifters, drunks and dropouts Quinn discovers throughout New York. The cityscape itself is flat, uniform, without depth, its repetitions and lack of features creating what Edward Relph called the placelessness of place. One of Quinn's walks is recorded by means of over three pages of street names, a *tour de force* which has been perceived as resistance rather than resignation. Interwoven with the numbered streets are items that would be found on a tourist map – the Flatiron Building, the Staten Island Ferry, Grand Central Station, Chinatown – that is, another futile attempt to totalise and 'know' the city.

The busy signal Quinn hears when he regularly attempts to phone Virginia Stillman imposes a regular pattern on the jumbled sounds of the city. His passage through the city streets appears random and unmotivated: at times he wanders haphazardly yet on his way to Third Avenue, he 'hooked', 'cut diagonally' and 'jutted'. The impression of purpose is illusory; moreover the postmodern city withholds its secrets from the detective. 'Blank concrete walls and reflecting glass windows reveal nothing of what takes place inside buildings: corporate activities take place "between the lines" whilst poverty is forced into the "margins".'[11]

Quinn's gaze, in Brian Jarvis's interpretation, is a symbol of electronic surveillance by bureaucratic and police organizations though the effect of the protagonist's spying has been to expose social injustice, the revelation of which impels him to become a dissenting under-consumer. So it is Jarvis's citation of Haug's allusion to the way commodities 'watch' us (turning the self into the third person, it should be added) that is most useful here.[12] Thus the city itself can be indicted as the physical representation of the economic and social relations of late capitalism. Quinn's downward mobility, however, causes him to merge with the city, the built environment of the throw-away society. Acquiescing in the status quo of wasteful capitalism is politically regressive. De Certeau can be similarly charged: renting as a response to the real estate bonanza is one thing; recommending individualism (freedom, autonomy) in preference to collectivity (power and oppression) is quite another, and, when implemented, has demonstrably calamitous consequences for disadvantaged city dwellers.

Social history has blocked the appearance of New York-based fictional detectives. The gang became in the nineteenth century the basic unit of social life among young men, and in the following century the term became standard among investigators of juvenile delinquency. Adult criminals preferred more impressive descriptions, euphemisms such as 'Cosa Nostra', the Family or simply 'the Organization'. The Mafia, which originated in New Orleans in the 1880s, features prominently in James Lee Burke's *The Neon Rain* (1987) and James Lochte's *Blue Bayou* (1992). In the latter the Benedettos are central to the narrative plot, but in each text the author is eager to demolish what Lochte terms that 'Godfather blood-is-thicker-than-vino mythology'. Didi Gee in *The Neon Rain* is a vicious, sentimental psychopath who used to keep a bloodstained baseball bat in the back of his convertible, and although the character of Reevie Benedetto with his Swiss education and his Athletic Club open to all races resembles that of the relatively complex Michael Corleone, he is equally amoral and ultimately another sociopath .

The Mafia emerged in New York during the same period, the late nineteenth century. In 1916 a war between the Mafia in Manhattan and the Camorra (Brooklyn) was a watershed in metropolitan crime whose history stretched from the underclass hoodlums of Five Points on the Lower East Side to the powerful Gambino family a century later. 'The Mob slipped into the regular life of the city, selling not just vice and booze and gambling but concrete, garbage collection and children's frocks, justice and politics, taxing what was built, trucked or carted away as though it was a second government.'[13]

In crime fiction the Mob has become associated specifically

with New York, to the extent that its power and influence are un-limited, spreading far beyond the spatial limits of Manhattan and Queens. Frankie King in Carl Hiassen's *Native Tongue* informs on members of Gotti's family and under the Witness Relocation Program sets up a theme park at North Key Largo near Miami. However, his cover is blown and he is killed by a fat, balding hitman from New York whose herringbone jacket and gold jewelry invite interpretation as the uniform of the tourist.

Counterparts of the hitman Lou (Rossiter) appear as body-guards in *Florida Straits* (1992). Emerging from a black Lincoln on to a Key West street to menace the book's hero Joey Goldman, these hoodlums from Queens in their blue shiny suits are movie caricatures. Significantly they have 'landlocked brains' so their dominance is only intermittent: when they drive away, 'the life of Key West surged back into the space they emptied'. In their next appearance they are at least provided with an appropriate setting: Mount Trashmore, a pyramid of garbage on nearby Stock Island whose shabby buildings (half-painted cinder block shacks), violence, drug dealing and general squalor insert a chilling echo of the urban nightmare.

Laurence Shames's crime novel is typically anti-urban but what makes it distinctive is its subversive challenge to New York coloni-alism. Joey Goldman's destiny is constrained by his ethnic duality: half-Jewish, he knows he can never succeed or be a full member of his mafioso father's family. Fleeing with his partner Sandra to tropical Key West he plans to 'map out the turf' and take over the rackets, unaware of the futility of 'carrying the neighbourhood around' with him. Mocked, insulted and threatened, he receives a salutary lesson from the retired godfather figure Bert 'the Shirt' d'Ambrosio. 'You don't just show up someplace and act like you're a goddam franchise, like you're opening a branch office of the Mob. Whaddya think, it's like fucking McDonald's?' Joey comes to real-ise the need to respond to local conditions and opportunities and articulates a central distinction: 'Up north the money comes outta the street, down here it comes outta the water.'[14]

The plot is impelled by his need to separate the two ways of life; if Florida cannot be entirely quarantined from New York , at least the resources it provides can be used to fulfil his 'family' obliga-tions. Joey takes to the water only to discover that at night it seems to disappear and the line between coast and water becomes a blur. The process of discarding his New York reference points is painful;

he expects channel markers to be as clear as the reflectors on the Brooklyn-Queens Expressway. He is surprised to discover that on charts of the ocean the land is blank. Yet emeralds miraculously do emerge from the water and Joey has somehow mapped his own secure future.

The Mob, and more specifically the Mafia, has generated a romantic image of crime, satisfying both individualist and collective desires.[15] The Godfather, in Mario Puzo's novel of that name (1969) and subsequently Coppola's films, is not merely the urban gangster as example of the American myth of success and social mobility. He is also a figure of confidence, responsibility and authority, a model to others and a guardian of a way of life. Since the text of The Godfather promotes the myth of infinite power, then the main representative of that power takes on a royal, priestly status, as much god as godfather. The literary and filmic materials provide a social alibi: the city is violent and corrupt as a result of criminal activities, particularly the criminal alliance between rich businessmen, politicians and the gangsters who control them. At the same time the violence and corruption with which the Mafia is identified can be disinfected by comparison with the assassination programmes of the CIA and by the sentimental justification of the family and its need for protection.

On the one hand the family offers kinship ties, loyalty, warmth and protection for the individual. On the other, as the symbolism is conveniently extended to the organisation, the tribal and ethnic culture of relationships, behaviour and codes, even religious belief, provide the organisation with its discipline and strength. The phenomenon of The Godfather (Parts I and II) in the early 1970s highlighted the failure of those institutions (including the American family) which had traditionally stood for stability and ethics: the church, the law, the education system, and the closely knit neighbourhood groups that helped to define the city's geography.

In Puzo's novel Michael Corleone justifies both the family and the life style of his father, explaining that while the rules of society are a barrier to Don Corleone's force and character, his own code of ethics is superior to the legal structures of that society. In Coppola's film the don is portrayed sympathetically by Marlon Brando as a gentle father figure, a supporter of capitalism, an opponent of drugs, and the source of honour and respect: in Brando's own description, a man of 'substance, tradition, dignity, refinement'. David Thomson poses (and answers) the question of The Godfather's immense popularity: 'we identify with the Corleones ... because their steady faith in social order allays our fears that the world is on the edge of decay and chaos.'[16]

The conflation of the family and the organised gang operates in a contradictory manner: the critique of the sterile soullessness of the modern corporation is ironic in view of the mob's own benevolent paternalism that operates to defer revelation of its exploitation and rapacity. There is a further irony in associating the ethnic family with big business, the culturally levelling phenomenon most responsible for endangering ethnic integrity.

Yet already in *The Godfather* the ethnic family is under strain in its attempts to meet the demands of the extended family. Brother kills brother; husband abandons wife. While *The Godfather III* was replaying the emotive expressiveness of its predecessors, other Hollywood films perceived the ethnic family itself as the site of psychosis and perverse relations and therefore doomed to destruction. In a striking reversal of gender relations, and coinciding with the emergence in the US of independent female private eyes in crime fiction, power is transferred to strong deadly women, roles often performed by Angelica Huston. The pertinent examples are *Prizzi's Honor* (1985) in which she arranges the deaths of her father and her ex-lover's wife, and *The Grifters* (1990) where she murders her son and his lover whom she impersonates after the killing.

The moralistic formula of gangster texts demanded antagonists such as federal agents or precinct cops. In New York fiction, the cop has become the principal representative – frequently an ambiguous one – of law and order. During the 1950s Chester Himes was persuaded to create as the protagonists of his hard-boiled detective stories two black 'Harlem sheriffs', Coffin Ed Johnson and Grave Digger Jones. Like their white police counterparts they are figures of social dominance and personal strength, but paradoxically as servants of an hierarchical system, their power is severely constrained. Their condition as Afro-Americans underlines this contradiction and motivates their anger and aggression, the kind of intense emotion kept simmering in Harlem by squalor and oppression.

The hard-boiled novel, Himes has argued, is a quintessential American product, 'plain and simple violence in narrative form'. Coffin Ed and Digger are hard, at times brutal, and their faces, especially the former's, bear the marks and scars of life on the ghetto streets, where the release of suppressed emotion often results in mutilation. Overbearing and vengeful, they are portrayed with a degree of naturalism, achieved through characterisation, speech and location, but they also function symbolically, successors to the 'bad nigger' of folklore, for example Stagolee. They demonstrate, in the early novels at least, that even the subordinated and impoverished can instil fear and terror.

It is not violence alone which identifies these texts as part of the hard-boiled tradition. Within their own milieu of absurd fury and destructiveness, Coffin Ed and Digger Jones are as much genre fantasies as Marlowe and the Continental Op: quick-thinking professionals, incorruptibly honest, loyal to each other and brave. Driven often by a central quest, the plots tend to imitate Hammett's *The Maltese Falcon*, recommended to Himes by Marcel Duhamel who commissioned the novels for 'La Série Noire'. The resemblance is closest in the first novel *For Love of Imabelle* (1957), (re-published as *A Rage in Harlem* (1985)) where the ore in the padlocked trunk turns out to be fool's gold. As in Hammett's novel the lure attracts villains to Harlem and generates capers, intrigues and savage, even spectacular violence on both personal and public levels. The generic nature of Himes's novels is underlined by a further connection: 'Himes' text embodies the key elements of the *film noir* genre as defined by Borde and Chaumeton: "unstable rapport among the members in a criminal gang ... dreamlike and erotic relations ... and manhunts that take place in the most unusual settings".[17]

Himes's policemen adopt a melodramatic perspective in Harlem, dividing the locals into good and evil, innocent and criminal. This ethical rigidity produces self-righteous judgements which are acted upon vigorously and – in the manner of Hammett's Op – excessively, impinging at times on both the guilty and the blameless. They save their wrath for those who prey on the community: muggers, burglars and racketeers. Villains who act as informers can count on temporary protection from the cops who make sure the addicts among them are regularly supplied with drugs. The nature of the system they represent and the irrational milieu they police necessitates, at times, methods such as these which breach regulations. Grave Digger and Coffin Ed exert control by means of a consuming rage which announces their toughness. But it is a rage that pervades the whole community, a pathology that is the product of frustration, prejudice and powerlessness.

The excess could be interpreted as a means of challenging aspects of the genre, assessing the authenticity of heroism in a venal society. 'Himes' detective fiction appears in a new critical light as a comic antigenre in which the "crime" derives from a capitalist world fragmented by racism and exploitation.'[18] So hard-boiled philosophy and the mystification of the romanticised detective are displaced by racial politics in a material world. As the cops survey the urban terrain of Harlem they record the human damage inflicted by racism: 'Blank-eyed whores stood on the street corners swapping obscenities with twitching junkies. Muggers and thieves slouched in dark doorways waiting for someone to rob; but there wasn't anyone but each other. Children ran down the street, the dirty street littered with rotting vegetables, uncollected garbage, battered garbage cans, broken glass, dog offal ...'[19] Yet an area close to irredeemable such as Eighth Avenue and 125th Street described in *Cotton Comes To Harlem* (1965) nevertheless includes decent families and 'honest laborers' whose condition as black underclass survivors the cops attempt to ameliorate.

Crimes are explained in a number of the Harlem novels but loose ends and bewilderment remain. In a variation which can be found elsewhere in hard-boiled fiction, Grave Digger deduces the murderer in *The Real Cool Killers* but refuses to surrender her to the Law, since the victim, a wealthy white sadist who liked to beat up black girls, deserved to die. Like Spade in *The Maltese Falcon*, Digger knows he must produce a fiction to fit the circumstances for the police commissioner and proposes that the big Greek, Ulysses Galen, was killed by a punk's zip gun. Since the killer was one of the abused black girls, the cop's action becomes one of racial solidarity. Only by bending the law can Harlem's detectives occasionally achieve a successful resolution. In *All Shot Up* (1960), the stolen money ($50,000) is seized by the two officers and sent to the New York Herald Tribune Fresh Air Fund which arranges summer vacations for city kids of all races.

Coffin Ed and Digger dispense justice on behalf of a poverty-stricken community threatened by violent criminal activities and oppressed by extremes of weather; the climate in the crime novels is split almost equally between paralysing cold and sweltering heat, conditions which, cranking up the tension, are yet another component of the urban nightmare. In the aptly named *The Heat's On* (1967), the multiplicity of violent acts and deaths produces a 'steaming bedlam' in the torrid ghetto.

In other New York crime literature too, intense suffocating heat becomes the cause and equivalent of emotions boiling over. Summer becomes a dangerous inferno; in Vera Caspary's *Laura*,

1942 (filmed in 1944), the city smells at different times like wash-ing-up water and rotten eggs, a warning of disease and a plague other than crime, as well as a premonition of apocalypse. Among others, Lewis Mumford observed that the city seemed bent on its own annihilation. As in the case of LA, a disaster discourse is con-structed comprising fire, riots, hunger, plague, smog blotting out light at noon, traffic, inadequate facilities in hospitals and schools, a decaying infrastructure and an insufficiency of air, sun or light.

Himes used his Afro-American perspective to convey the dis-jointedness, the messy and turbulent atmosphere of the Harlem community. The surreal dynamism of this teeming ghetto world with its flamboyant, ribald citizens is rendered in a graphic style drawing upon laconic speech forms and Afro-American vernacular. In *My Life of Absurdity*, Himes maintained that he never actually knew how an inhabitant of Harlem lived, and he claimed that he was as much of a tourist there as 'a white man from downtown changing his luck'. His self-proclaimed ignorance of Harlem was exaggerated: in the detective novels, the city within a city is height-ened but recognizable, its details the result of observation and frequent walking. His knowledge of the criminal world, its styles, its spoken language, and of the lives of ghetto dwellers in other American cities, especially Cleveland, Ohio, was extensive. Thus specific novels focus on a different aspect of urban crime, of frauds and thefts that rob the already dispossessed: professional gambling (*The Crazy Kill*) (1959); drug dealing (*The Heat's On*); religious scams (*The Big Gold Dream*) .

The fictional Harlem is a self-contained society: the reader encounters its restaurants, foods, musical entertainment, churches, funeral parlours, pool rooms, clubs and tenements as well as its celebrated landmarks, the Apollo Theatre, Blumstein's Department Store and Small's Paradise. Despite the superficial 'concrete jungle' similarity, it contrasts in spirit and social perspective with another self-contained urban region: Isola in the police novels of Ed McBain. The milieu of these narratives is fragmented and individualistic; furthermore, the perspective is naturalistic, with the stoicism of human beings the characteristic response to the hostility of weather and the city itself. Greed and exploitation based on racial division are concealed or avoided in a dismissal of politics and economics. The fictionalisation of New York as Isola turns it into the universal modern city, alienating and unalterable. Himes at least locates his territory geographically:

Looking Eastward from the towers of Riverside Church, perched ... on the high banks of the Hudson river, in a valley far below, waves of gray rooftops distort the perspective like the surface of the sea. Below the surface, in the murky waters of fetid tenements, a city of black people who are convulsed in desperate living, like the voracious churnings of millions of hungry cannibal fish.[20]

Himes's vertical spatiality is a visual image of the intimidation and victimisation suffered by Harlem, where imprisoned in the valley black Americans grotesquely prey on each other. Although its people are deprived, sinful and resilient, black America's capital, like Chandler's Los Angeles, is enigmatic, intricate and continuously fascinating. In representing this section of the city Himes captures the sights of shop windows and graffiti, the sounds of jazz from neighbourhood bars, augmented by car horns, radios and semi-public arguments, and, in *The Heat's On* (1967) the smells of 'sizzling barbecue, fried hair, exhaust fumes, rotting garbage, cheap perfumes, unwashed bodies ... and all the dried-up odours of poverty.'[21]

Manthia Diawara has made a significant distinction between fictional public spheres in Harlem while noting the implications for black identity. Certain locations such as police stations, one of which, it can be said, serves as collective hero in the 87th Precinct novels, colonise the black life world, permitting only the reproduction of such black subjects as whores, thieves and other transgressors in need of regulation. In less formal places, bars, dance halls, bookie joints and the streets themselves, space exists for the construction of black culture and of individual identity through that culture. Within this environment Diawara selects the lawbreaker (such as Gus Parsons) as style model and hero in the community, 'the first to challenge the status quo'. 'The lawbreakers draw black people into the informal sector by keeping alive the dream of becoming rich promptly, and circumventing the colonizing systems.'[22] But as Diawatha properly maintains, *A Rage in Harlem* is a materialist text; just as Harlemites are vulnerable to promises of 'tickets to heaven' by Father Divine and other religious hucksters, so the naïve Jackson, with his wad of $10,000 is manipulated by Gus, with his smooth pitch about stock in a gold mine. In his turn Gus becomes rapidly and fatally the victim of Harlem's rage, anarchy and random brutality.

The details of a crowded, colourful city provide the anchor for the exuberance of fantasy. In his essay 'City of Harlem' (1962)

Leroi Jones reported that the mythology of the ghetto supplied different images, one vibrant and joyous, the other more melancholy, the focus of 'every crippling human vice'. Yet Harlem as Jones insisted eludes definitions, changing constantly, questioning the stereotypes of glamour and desperation. In that 'milling population of preachers and politicians, sober matriarchs and mock religious prophets, pimps and their chippies, drug pushers and wheel thieves, transvestites and conmen, and shysters of every kind and sex' anything might happen.[23] Many of the conmen are preachers ranging from the contemptible to the charismatic, all of them phoney, on the make and trailing a meretricious glamour. Himes's Harlem is subjected to racketeering, drug-dealing and hustling in general, so tension, fear and violence suffuse the various texts.

New York's black community has been called Southern in its memories and its culture: *The Crazy Kill* contains a complete soul food menu. In *Cotton Comes to Harlem* (1965) Himes juxtaposes two political projects one of which is the racist movement known as Back-to-the-Southland and led by the neo-Confederate Colonel Calhoun. This is symbolised by a bale of cotton carrying suggestions of slavery, which more or less describes the conditions awaiting those Harlemites who join up. Black militancy is represented by the despicable Deke O'Malley's Back-to Africa movement, a coded reference to Marcus Garvey's nationalist organisation in the 1920s. At the book's satisfying conclusion an old junk collector does travel to Ghana with the $87, 000 he finds in the cotton bale, the money stolen from the O'Malley Group's 'Last Chance Rally' by the Colonel's men.

Closure, providing an image of temporary success, is particularly important in minority literature. Echoing the ending of *All Shot Up*, a deal is struck so that the robbed Harlem families will receive $87,000 (from Back-to-the-Southland) while Calhoun and his nephew, guilty of racial murder, are allowed to evade justice by fleeing to Alabama. Himes is aware of the pathologies sustained in the racist South; for American blacks it represented racism and economic hardship, but it was also the site of family history and roots. By 1991, decades after the enactment of civil rights legislation, the denouement of Bill Dukes' film version of *For Love of Imabelle – A Rage in Harlem –* returns the principal characters Jackson and Imabelle, the 'natural-born *amante*' and prototype for *femmes fatales* elsewhere in the books, to the South, a haven from the city ghetto and its dangerous frenzies.

The limits of justice for blacks in the American city became increasingly obvious to Himes, and this theme is developed in the ambitious hard-boiled narrative *Blind Man With a Pistol* (1969), a de-centred, prophetic anti-novel in which the failure of the genre is part of the meaning. Harlem, which in *Plan B* ((1993), (1983) in French) experiences an Afro-American revolution, is described as completely anarchic, overwhelmed by meaningless violence. Its squalor and chaos are measured against a montage which nostalgically reconstructs an earlier Harlem, settled and respectable; at the centre of this urban pastoral is sited the old Theresa Hotel where Booker T. Washington, Billie Holiday, Josephine Baker and many other black celebrities stayed.

The cops' investigations are blocked because they would uncover an interracial homosexual scandal embarrassing to the white establishment. So the extreme point of absurdity is reached: crime can no longer be solved, for criminality is all-pervasive and accelerated by social decay. Similarly the disease of institutional racism in the ghetto is too advanced for any remedy.

Grave Digger and Coffin Ed here are ineffective comic characters with greying hair and middle-aged spread who move through Harlem like ghosts in a spectral car. (Similar disfigurations of their characters will take place in the movie *A Rage in Harlem*.) Farcical humour abounds; as riots and demonstrations proliferate, they can no longer impose order and are left standing half-dressed after a Molotov cocktail incinerates their car and singes their clothes. At 'the Mecca of Harlem', Seventh Avenue and 125th Street, parades representing different ideologies converge and collide in a narrative with sufficient references to Black Power and Malcolm X. The Black Muslim Michael X tells them they no longer count 'in the overall pattern'.

The parable of the blind man with a gun shooting indiscriminately in the New York subway provides the appropriate epilogue, a representation, as Himes's preface warns, of the unorganised violence that connects the Middle East, Vietnam and America's ghettoes. Closure is rejected as Himes's black detectives adjust to impotence and irrationality, taking pot-shots at fat rodents in a building on 125th Street demolished by urban renewal. Riots break out once more renewing the discourse of urban calamity.

The text of Jerome Charyn's *The Isaac Quintet*, permeated by energy, spirituality and linguistic invention, resists such rhetoric while acknowledging the turbulence of New York's streets and the ubiquity of crime. Ethnic multiplicity and complexity provide the racial and cultural space for Charyn's police detective, Isaac Sidel, a chess-playing ex-Stalinist who admires Eisenstein and Hammett. His stamping ground is the Lower East Side where Jews, Irish, Hispanics, Chinese and mulattoes mingle, where his mother who befriended Arabs and Puerto Ricans in preference to Jews has a junk shop, and where he can buy horseradish and onion bread. Like the rest of Manhattan it is vulnerable to change, the old Forsyth synagogue, for instance, having become a Puerto Rican 'Templo Adventista' still with the Star of David in the circular window.

Charyn feels a psychic attachment to the Lower East Side though his own roots are in the Bronx, an area he hands over to a gang of Marrano pickpockets from Peru who function as Sidel's antagonists in the first three narratives. Isaac's Irish wife is also Bronx-based but makes her real estate profits outside the city in Florida; essentially the territories of the novel – Manhattan and the Bronx – are inhabited by criminals, politicos and cops, both good and bad.

A thorough metropolitan, Isaac sees other cities in terms of New York. In Paris he can 'sniff out' Madison Avenue in the bakeries and jewellery shops off the rue Hamelin. Eccles Street, where Joyce sited Leopold Bloom in *Ulysses*, is like parts of the Bronx, 'bombed-out territories and a few pubs'. Isaac wanders listlessly in Dublin, a cop armed with a hairbrush. At the height of his power he commands the Lower East Side with his own network of informers and sidekicks. Merchants rush out to kiss his hand and folk in the candy stores wave to him. Part of that power and authority is derived from a knowledge of the city's streets, an ability to 'nose out the contours of a neighbourhood' anywhere in Manhattan. In contrast, he is disoriented by 'that trapping of streets' in Galway City, and on the coast he is mystifyed by country roads where the only landmarks are stones and trees.

Nor does the Deputy Commissioner's adaptation to and control of Lower Manhattan extend to the Bronx, an acknowledgement that, despite a certain amount of ethnic blending, zones and identities are strictly defined. This is particularly the case with the tribal Guzmanns, united by customs, beliefs and territory. Realising he cannot ensnare them with 'old coordinates and shitty spies' Isaac resigns his post, spreads rumours of his misdoings and becomes Papa Guzmann's henchman, but to no avail. The payoff for him is a tapeworm, a black tongue and no arrests. In addition he can no longer consider the Lower East Side his patrimony, a change signified by the abandonment of the old limestone Police Headquarters on Centre Street for a huge red monolith in Chinatown. 'Isaac had fallen out of touch with the landladies, grocers and pensioners of his bishopric. The Guzmanns had pecked under his sideburns and devoured the white meat in his head. Isaac stumbled through the East Side like an unbrained bear.'[24]

Charyn's urban vision is the characteristic one of the city as jungle but distorted into an exotic, bizarre expressionistic panorama, full of nightmares, violence and transformations. Just as the mysterious city challenges the voyeur and the wanderer to make their readings, so Isaac who has been described as a sequence of alternate identities, contributes to that mystery by adopting a variety of disguises. Periodically his job demands that he disappear into the city's anonymity: when he cannot discover what is happening on the street, it is time to go underground, to become 'the old man of Forty-Seventh Street'.

This role externalises the loneliness of the detective who prefers to sit alone in Hubert's deli on Essex Street than to rub shoulders with mafiosi (and other DCIs) in the clamhouses on Mulberry and Grand. His triumphs are always hollow. Those he loves, such as blue-eyed Coen, and the whore Annie Powell are snatched away by death. In what Charyn perceives as a fragmented and violent world riddled with dreams, Isaac's achievement is survival and the mere illusion of mastery.

Isaac's sortie underground does not take him into the nightmarish, fetid world introduced in 'Urban discourse', where the residents of the lower depths are represented, in the perspective of social pathology, as the equivalent of a human zoo. Such an alien subculture, distinctively other, inhabits the infrastructure of New York. Within the knotted tendrils of telephone cables, power lines, steam pipes and gas mains there exists a parallel city. In the tunnels under Grand Central and Penn Stations and other literally suburban parts of New York, the homeless form their own groupings (by age, race etc.) and establish codes of behaviour. Benny Profane, a character in Pynchon's novel *V* (1963) takes a job hunting alligators in the New York sewers, the association of 'underground' and crime being made through Benny's co-workers, Italian-Americans from the East Side. The association however is parodic for the street gangs have no geographical territories. 'The Street', from which Benny learns nothing, is as two-dimensional as its representation in little red guide books.

Infrastructural settings in film, drama and television usually act as a sign for the crime narrative, although in the early example of Fritz Lang's *Metropolis* (1927), the Gothic landscape of cathedral, charnel house and catacombs provides the setting for economic crime; the industrialist's son descends to discover the subterranean workers who keep the futuristic city functioning. The commercial aspect of the underground is explored by Chester Himes in *Run Man Run*, though the location is the basement of Schmidt and Schindler's luncheonette where black porters load garbage cans on to the lift for collection. It is in this area that the protagonist Jimmy, one of the porters, is pursued by the crazed white cop Walker whose flapping trench coat and manic, skeleton-like face recalls the Phantom of the Opera (and by extension the underground labyrinth of ramps, stairways and tunnels that leads to his cavernous den). The basements and the adjoining corridors become for Jimmy 'a world of black dark horror', where the noise of garbage cans, used as weapons, is not only ear-shattering but masks the sound of Walker's silenced gun. Released into above-ground Manhattan, Jimmy attempts on a bus journey to read the city, to gauge the emotions of those around him, an effort obliterated by the recurring sense of dread. Food at the corner of 149th Street provides a temporary respite. But a sighting of Walker awakens him to the knowledge of his lack of protection in the violent city, his vulnerability compounded anywhere in the nation by his skin.

Only in Harlem, close to the Theresa Hotel whose bookstore displays works by Richard Wright, Langston Hughes and Claude McKay can Jimmy feel not only protected but empowered.

> *Black* was a big word in Harlem. No wonder so many Negro people desired their own neighbourhood, he thought. They feel safe; there was safety in numbers.
> The idea of a white maniac hunting him down to kill seemed as remote as yesterday's dream. If he had seen Walker at the moment he would have walked up to him and knocked out his teeth.[25]

Nourished by hog maws, turnip greens, speckled peas and chili sauce, Jimmy's personality becomes mean and dangerous; he is ready to grab Walker's head and twist it off.

As early as 1959 when *Run Man Run* appeared in France (*Dare-Dare*), Brock the decent white detective has an apocalyptic vision of a ruined, consumed New York. In 1979, the movie *The*

Warriors featured whole gangs finding refuge in the subways which, like the sewers, offer hideouts and escape channels. But they can also harbour malign plots: Lex Luthor's lair in *Superman* (1978) is located beneath Grand Central Station. In the 1980s, movies with underground settings moved towards horror and science fiction genres, populating the subterranean areas with robots and freaks. John Carpenter's cyberpunk exercise, *Escape from New York* (1981), made in St Louis as New York's streets were considered too dangerous, envisages a crime-ridden future in which the wasteland of Manhattan Island has become a walled prison. Here it is the criminally insane who issue from beneath the damp, dark streets. In *C.H.U.D.* (1984), a paranoid movie involving government secrecy, toxic waste under New York creates cannibalistic mutants among the homeless residents.

The antithesis of the underground lair is the skyscraper. In the Twenties and Thirties Hugh Ferris an ex-architect designed futuristic images of the metropolis, fantasies of the air with skyscrapers housing golf courses and hosting masked balls on their roofs. The hero's perspective in *Batman Returns* as the penguins invade Gotham City shows the value of the aerial shot for Hollywood's urban films. Down below at street level and inside the underworld the city is bleak and dark. De Certeau gives a reminder that what is seen from on high are mere *cadavres* giving rise to the contemplation that the totalising panoramic view is akin to the vision of the city as dead. Later the New York World's Fair 'Democracity' was enclosed in Ferris's Perisphere, but the sensation of suspension and floating was only an illusion. Ferris literally came down to earth, relocating the future beneath the ground, and in 1942 proposed rebuilding New York in vaults under the New Jersey Palisades: the city redefined as massive air raid shelter.

NOTES

1   J. P. Sartre, 'Manhattan: the Great American Desert' (1946) in Alexander Klein (ed.), *The Empire City: A Treasury of New York* (Freeport, New York, Books for Libraries Press, 1971), p. 453.

2   E. McBain, *Downtown* (London, New York, Guild Publishing, 1989), pp. 233–4.

3   McBain, *Downtown*, p. 225.

4   /S./ Munt/ ' "Somewhere over the Rainbow ... " Postmodernism and the Fiction of Sarah Schulman' in /S./Munt/ (ed.), *New Lesbian Criti-*

cism; Literary and Cultural Readings (New York, London, Harvester Wheatsheaf, 1992), p. 40. This invaluable essay is the most informative and perceptive examination of Schulman's texts.

5   T. Wolfe, *The Bonfire of the Vanities* (London, Picador, 1988), pp. 66, 96.

6   A. Vachss, *Hard Candy* (New York, Signet, 1990), p. 11.

7   Wolfe, *Bonfire*, pp. 501, 506.

8   M. de Certeau, 'Walking in the City', in S. During (ed.), *The Cultural Studies Reader* (London , New York, Routledge, 1993), pp.153–4.

9   P. Auster, *City of Glass* in *The New York Trilogy* (London, Faber, 1988), pp. 8–9.

10   Jarvis, 'Crime in the "City of Glass" ', p. 36.

11   *Ibid.*, p. 41.

12   W. F. Haug, *Critique of Commodity Aesthetics : Appearance, Sexuality and Advertising in Capitalist Society* (Cambridge, Polity Press, 1984) is noted in Jarvis. See pp. 36, 44.

13   M. Pye, *Maximum City: the Biography of New York* (London, Picador, 1993), p. 238.

14   L. Shames, *Florida Straits* (New York, Dell, 1992), pp. 68, 102.

15   The Mafia discourse, postulating not only the fantasy of an all-powerful criminal organisation but also the centrality of Italian-American gangsters, became increasingly potent with the appearance of Puzo's novel and its many literary and filmic imitators. For further details and an exposition of the governmental interests this discourse served, see M. Woodiwiss, 'Crime's global reach' in F. Pearce and M. Woodiwiss (eds.), *Global Crime Connections* (Basingstoke, Macmillan, 1993).

16   D. Thomson, *America in the Dark* (London, Hutchinson, 1978), p. 189.

17   M. Diawara, 'Noir by Noirs: Toward a New Realism in Black Cinema' in J. Copjec (ed.), *Shades of Noir* (London, New York, Verso, 1993), p. 265. The French text referred to is *Panorama du film noir américain* (1955).

18   G. H. Muller, *Chester Himes* (Boston, Twayne Publishers) 1989, p. 85.

19   C. Himes, *Cotton Comes to Harlem* (Harmondsworth, Penguin, 1974), p. 47.

20   C. Himes, *A Rage in Harlem* (London, Allison and Busby, 1985), p. 93.

21   C. Himes, *The Heat's On* (London, Panther, 1969), p. 28.

22   Diawara, 'Noir by Noirs', p. 272.

23   A. R. Lee, 'Harlem on my mind : Fictions of a Black Metropolis' in G. Clarke (ed), *The American City: Literary and Cultural Perspectives* (London/New York; Vision Press/St Martins Press, 1988), p. 80.

24   J. Charyn, *The Isaac Quartet* (London, Zomba Books, 1984), p. 302.

25   C. Himes, *Run Man Run* (London, Allison and Busby, 1990), p. 152.

5

MIAMI

Billy Wilder's 1959 film *Some Like It Hot* associated Chicago with night, violence and swift death. Miami by contrast, stood for sunshine, vitality and fun. Such a polarisation was a fictional device as the film tacitly admitted when the plot moved the hoodlums south in search of the two musicians who had witnessed the St. Valentine's Day massacre. Although Miami was an exclusive resort in the 1920s, it already had an unsavoury history comprising pervasive and chronic racism consolidated by settlers from the north, widespread Mafia activity in which Meyer Lansky was prominent, and its adoption during Prohibition by Al Capone, an 'antique dealer'. In the Depression gunfights between G-men and smugglers were common. So Miami's assumption of the title 'Murder Capital USA' in the early 1980s was in reality an exercise in continuity.

The prevalence of criminality, intriguingly mixed in with the Florida postcard attributes of surf, sun, beach and lush tropical plants made Miami as dangerous and exciting as Chicago. Miami, like New Orleans, was exotic by virtue of its links with other races, languages and cultures. In addition, it was literally colourful, capitalising on the exuberant surfaces of its three- and four-storey South Beach Art Deco hotels which entranced Elmore Leonard and provided the setting for *LaBrava*. The writer was attracted not only by the windblown charm of the buildings but also by the mixture of residents with little in common, who were mainly Jewish ex-garment workers from New York and refugees from Latin America.

In TV's *Miami Vice* the colours are pastel (such as cotton candy pink), and flourescent, constitutive of a city that is post-industrial, vibrant and stylistically ambitious. The artificial settings are complemented by indigenous, atmospheric ones: 'Teeming with images of nature – parrots, flamingos, water and speed, women's bodies, flaunting sensuality – Miami is our heart of darkness.'[1]

Maurice Zola, the old hotelier in Leonard's *LaBrava* (1983), repeats the rumour that the east bank of the Apalachicola River between Bristol (where Noah may have built the Ark) and Chatahoochee is the site of the original Garden of Eden. Miami is both heart of darkness and fallen world: its paradisal luxury, its oceanside ambience of yachts and seaplanes predicated on credit, the arms trade, and drug sales – the profits from which have criminalized businessmen, politicians and police officers. Moral distinctions between commodities are obliterated in a democracy of desire and consumerism, an aspect made prominent in *Miami Vice* where the environments echo fashion magazines and car commercials.

Unpacking the connotations of the title of Michael Mann's popular series – 'Miami Vice' meaning both crime and the police squad – reveals yet again the equivalence of law/order and deviance. The pleasure obtained from the equation derives from the programme's formal preoccupations, sometimes summarised as its MTV aesthetic, and its exotic Miami backdrop of affluence, cool glistening colours and tropical scenery. *Miami Vice* displays a measure of 1930s-style social criticism, unearthing corruption among the rich, sophisticated and publicly respectable. A similar intertextuality can be found elsewhere in the Miami discourse, for instance in Elmore Leonard's novel *Stick* (1983), which includes a mansion sufficiently grand to rival earlier monuments belonging to the Sternwoods or Grayles.

> An assortment of low modules stuck together, open sides and walls of glass set at angles, the grounds dropping away from the house in gradual tiers, with wide steps that might front a museum leading down to the terraced patio and on to the swimming pool. A sweep of manicured lawn extended to a boat dock and a southwest view of Biscayne Bay, downtown Miami standing in rows of highrises beyond.[2]

On the other hand its cop heroes no longer embrace the poverty which, in Marlowe and other PIs, accompanies that perspective. For their undercover work Crockett and Tubbs parade the same clothes and commodities – the expensive automobiles, the Rolex watch, the Italian suits – as the authentic drug traffickers they impersonate under the names of Burnett and Cooper. Crockett's Ferrari Daytona once belonged to a cocaine dealer, and in the pilot episode his ex-wife describes cops and crooks as two sides of the same coin: 'You're all players, Sonny. You get high on the action.' The danger for the cops as for the rest of society in Miami, is addiction to crime not to drugs, as Sonny recognises when he calls 'selling out' the American dream. Elmore Leonard also reduces the moral distance between his protagonists and villains through alternating points of view, and by displacing the traditional hunt for the killer. In novels such as *Glitz* a mutual monitoring takes place as the two principals continually circle each other.

Relentlessly, drugs and vice are associated with a capitalistic society in which criminals thrive on drugs, and politicians and lawmen prosper from the drug traffic which has been fostered by the Law itself. As the Colombian drug baron Banda-Conchesa explains in Richard Hoyt's *Marimba* (1992), the war on drugs is a bureaucrat's dream, beyond criticism and justifying frequent new operations that require subventions of taxpayers' money. 'In "Miami Vice" the boundaries of illegitimate economic activity cross and merge. Weapons and drug deals are inseparable from white-collar crime and government cover-up.'³ The free market and its surrounding culture are ultimately self-destructive since they are steeped in greed, materialism, addiction and sexual immorality. However, potential radicalism is thwarted in familiar ways. Politics is formally dissipated by the domination of style and surface, and by the universal nature of corruption.

In this revision of the theatre of the absurd, duplicity, drug-related vice and commodification extend vertically through groups and institutions, influencing both public and private life, and horizontally filling the city's spaces, sometimes seductively, sometimes appallingly. This spatial incursion is shocking when the vertical process mentioned becomes dramatically horizontal, and the domestic space of the family home is invaded by a band of armed men, terrorising and humiliating people, assaulting or killing them and their animals. Meanwhile, back on the streets, good and bad become indistinguishable. 'This is Miami, pal', Crockett tells Tubbs, 'where you can't even tell the players without a program.' Ricardo Tubbs with his mixed ancestry, Afro and Hispanic, has no trouble becoming a 'player' in this multicultural society.

Although the work of Crockett and Tubbs increasingly reveals a national dimension to vice, foreigners, especially in the form of unassimilated exiles, are often stigmatised as crooks. The issue of social amelioration is dislodged by that of endemic crime in the ghetto or individual moral weakness. The familiar naturalistic symbols of plants and animals are employed and the combination of drugs, sex and violence invokes the metaphor of disease. Vice becomes a plague, the result of a virus originating outside the USA and now out of control in beseiged Miami. Vietnam signifies as a source of disintegration and current danger, while Haiti registers the fear of AIDS.

Miami Vice demonstrates that postmodernity, responsible for both wealth and immiseration on a global scale, has a particular reference to the USA. Flooded by European and Japanese goods and established as the dumping ground for Third World cocaine, Miami functions as the victim of an overwhelming natural force, impelling American economic and social decline. If circulation is an intrinsic part of the modern city, the circulation of, and traffic in commodities, especially illegal ones, serves to define the image of Miami. Drugs are central to the perception of invasive tidal waves or epidemics so that the 'war on drugs' takes the form of violent repulsion. Frightening indicators of social chaos, they ironically link the economic extremes of society in *Miami Vice* creating a lawless yet cohesive 'community' of desire and pleasure.

For Crockett and Tubbs, however, the pleasures of dandyism and consumerism are dulled by the ubiquitous nature of urban crime. The absence of narrative resolution, the shadowy morality, the frequency of scenes of mourning and pathos, the detectives' own crises of conscience and identity, the unfocused, hallucinatory ambience of Miami – cumulatively these produce a morose melancholia, which only the rigid stoicism of their boss Lieutenant Castillo can resist.

By the 1980s Miami and Florida had taken over from Los Angeles and Southern California in the American consciousness as lotus land, the main centre for opportunity and easy living. Still evolving and changing, Miami promoted itself as the pioneer centre of a new international arena of leisure, a waking dream of tropical romance.

That dream would increasingly partake of violence and criminality. Miami, a clearing house for immigrants and refugees was becoming an entrepôt for illicit goods, a city of touts and pimps and middlemen, importing or distributing whatever prospective buyers wished to acquire. Its internationalism would embrace not only cafe society Europeans and, more recently, fashion models but Colombian cocaine cowboys, French-speaking Haitians and the 'marielitos' tossed out from Mariel by Castro and described as the most ruthless criminals ever seen in the USA. Many of those involuntary immigrants were addicts, prostitutes and homosexuals; among the rest were large numbers of petty crooks, usually vicious, and about two thousand hard core villains who would send Miami's crime figures through the roof. By 1991, in *Native Tongue*, novelist Carl Hiassen could suggest that Miami was a prime location site for large numbers of federal stool pigeons because in South Florida 'any dirtbag would blend in smoothly with the existing riffraff'.

The broken, fragmentary narratives of Elmore Leonard are one formal means of representing Miami's diversity. They have a particular purpose in relativising morality but, like the nineteenth-century European novel, they construct multiple, miscellaneous experience as urban, with social encounters shown to be contingent and arbitrary. In fictional Miami as in Dickens' London, ' unknown and unacknowledged relationships, profound and decisive connections, definite and committing recognitions and avowals are as it were forced into consciousness'.[4]

Other public events contributed towards the construction of the city's violent image. The Liberty City riots were yet another example of the brutality engendered by Southern racism, while the Suniland shoot-out exposed the dark underside of Middle America. Matix and Platt were army veterans from the Midwest, patriotic, garden-loving, pious suburbanites who killed their wives for the insurance, Matix setting the pattern in Ohio, his new buddy Platt following suit in Miami and celebrating his wealth by taking his kids to Disneyworld. The two men used the flamboyant cars of young Hispanic males they had murdered for armed robberies; they were finally cornered and shot in a black and gold Chevrolet Monte Carlo. In Elmore Leonard's novel *Stick* (1984), Chucky Gorman, a drugs dealer, warns Moke, a young redneck working for a Cuban outfit, that he has seen 'white boys ... take on that greaseball strut, that curl to the lip and land in a federal correction facility for showing off'. Part of the fascination of the Miami novel is this clash of cultures and the way power depends on cultural images and their manipulation.

Nestor, Chucky's associate in crime, is Hispanic Cuban but stories tag him as part Lengua Indian from Paraguay, 'raised on the alkaline flats and fed spider eggs' to make him evil. He is able to terrify Chucky through references to *santería* and animal sacrifice, having known for a long time that 'gods can scare the shit out of anyone'.[5] Nestor apart, Cubans usually fill the reductive roles of

small-time hoods in these texts and are the target of racist senti-
ments ('that greaser goon Chavez', 'fucking Cuban hotshot').
Cundo Rey the glitzy go-go artist in *LaBrava* (1983) at least gets to
say, 'I steal cars in darkness, I dance in lights' but needs little invitation to 'act crazy'. Jesus Bernal, the incompetent letter-bomber in
Carl Hiassen's *Tourist Season* (1986), is a similar figure ending up
as the weird Cuban, a mixture of clown and loose cannon. Drug
smugglers in TV series and fiction are usually Jamaican, Haitian or
Colombian; brutal and psychotic, they invite the extermination
required by colonialist ideology.

Central casting might have selected Matix and Platt as straight
arrow agents of law enforcement. They lived and died in suburban,
churchgoing Kendall, the location of the expensive condo where
Freddy 'Junior' Frenger, the psychopathic protagonist of Charles
Willeford's *Miami Blues* (1985), holes up with his 'platonic' wife
Susan. The apartment complex in the novel exemplifies the contradictions and volatility of Miami life in the early 1980s. Chic and
tropical, it is for the most part unpainted or unfinished because construction prices and interest rates on loans have risen. A Cuban
rides around in a jeep to stop vandalism.

Miami, with its lush vegetation, its aura of enchantment and its
shimmering skyline overlooking Biscayne Bay and the Atlantic
Ocean may, at least to the tourist, seem the antithesis of the murky
streets of depravity and violence found in *film noir* and the classic
hard-boiled thriller. As Sharon Zukin observes, the city in *Miami
Vice* is one 'in which no one works at productive tasks, a city where
industry is relegated to slimy backwater piers along the Miami
River. "Miami Vice" is service-sector Miami, where money is made
by "deals", not work ...'[6] Miami, a city of neighbourhoods and
shopping malls, also lacks the functioning downtown of skyscrapers
associated with older versions of metropolis. Downtown in Miami
means outlets for jewellery and cheap electronics aimed at Hispanic
tourists.

There remains a degree of graphic social realism in the writings
of Leonard and Willeford, and even *Miami Vice* with its emphasis
on contemporary fashions moves its cops through those familiar
urban spaces which signify the extremes of affluence and squalor.
'Crockett and Tubbs go out from their office and down into the
city's recesses and labyrinths: bars, pool halls, opium dens, flop-
houses, brothels on the one hand; the opulent homes, pools, yachts
and parties of the super-rich on the other.'[7]

In the contemporary crime novel, notably the Miami variety, violence is not restricted to private enclaves and the underworld. When Freddy Frenger in *Miami Blues* snaps the finger of a Hare Krishna supplicant at Miami airport, observers break into applause and laughter. The wounded beggar who dies of shock turns out to be the brother of the young hooker with whom Frenger shacks up. Susan and Marty Waggoner were saving up for a Burger King franchise and middle class materialism in Okeechobee: 'He'll be the day manager and I'll manage nights. We'll build a house on the lake, get us a speedboat and everything.' The demise of Marty who was cheating the Hare Krishnas is ironic; as a child he liked to bend back his sister's fingers. When puberty struck the pair, he made her pregnant. So much for the American Dream. But it has appeal for Frenger too. "What I want is a regular life. I want to go to work in the morning or maybe at night, and come home to a clean house, and a decent dinner, and a loving wife like you.'[8] At such moments Frenger performs bewilderingly as the suburban psychopath, dream and nightmare made inextricable.

Sometimes the dream/nightmare conjunction has an historical basis. Heroin was smuggled from Vietnam in the bodies of dead soldiers; in an episode of *Miami Vice* an attractive air hostess who needs money for a BMW agrees to transport drug samples inside her body. The cocaine leaks resulting in her agonised death, the penetration of the body by disease supplying the subtext. The lack of fixity in Miami, its pleasurable tropical blur gives rise to an amorphousness that offers space in which to hustle and rob, to maim others or yourself. Criminality in the Miami text is closely linked to lack of place and roots, lack of traditions except that of crime itself. One consequence of the city's status as haven for thousands of transients and travellers is the decline of family life, that centred world which often formed the structure of the nineteenth century novel and would later write the scenario for tension and violence in the novels of Ross Macdonald. Urban atomisation renders more difficult the role of the hard-boiled detective such as Marlowe, the classic loner ranged against decadent or corrupt groupings.

Watching 'Family Feud' on television, Frenger observes that there are no mothers and fathers on the show, only cousins, uncles and perhaps a kid borrowed from the neighbours. The cynical reflection of the Police Officer Hoke Moseley on the Waggoners makes an epitaph for the Reaganite Eighties, and for Miami: 'That's some family isn't it? Incest, prostitution, fanaticism, software.'⁹

Instead of family life, the Miami crime novel produces representations of lifestyles connected somewhere by crime. Just as a palm tree, jacuzzi and red staircase seem suspended in space within the reflective façade of Arquitectonica's Brickell Avenue condominium, so characters in books by Leonard, James Hall and Joseph Koenig float in their individual ways, as though acknowledging Miami's rivers, oceans, storms and flourescent swimming pools. Koenig's *Floater* (1986) is a corpse; the book's major criminal dumps one, but ends up the same way in the Tamiani canal. Miami's topography functions as a watery cemetery. Although the Everglades bleed Miami from the rear-view mirror as motorists on the Tamiani Trail approach the Big Cypress swamp and the Gulf Coast, the wilderness area shares in the ambivalence and menace of the city. Alice in *Floater* calls her family hunting lodge with its Spanish moss in the front yard and its freshwater lagoon in the back 'the honeymoon cottage', but her partner Norodny drowns his first victim in an Everglades guest house. Swamps and marshes have traditionally been considered places of horror and sickness in western culture. If the Everglades National Park supplies a mythic image of prelapsarian nature, therefore, it is also a source of Southern Gothic, a miasmal, haunted setting of swampland, mosquitoes, alligators and white trash.

A discourse of the Gothic can function as the expressive medium of a nostalgic, even obsessive environmentalism. Skip Wiley's self-imposed mission in Carl Hiassen's *Tourist Season* is to wreak vengeance on the boosters, wheeler-dealers, bankers and developers who, with bulldozers and dredgers , have not only turned the city of Miami into 'Newark with palm trees' but have made it an environmental disaster area, summed up in a separate Miami text by Jeb, a hitman, car thief and rapist as 'a tropical city in unrinsed water, where the blue air shimmers with diesel fumes and the grey water thickens like syrup from saturated waste'.¹⁰

Ecology is also fundamental to James Hall's *Under Cover of Daylight* (1987). Its action takes place largely in the islands of the Florida Keys, but the characters and tone, and the congested, sprawling landscape of Southern Florida where vegetation, marshland, freeways, suburbia and seashore are intermingled, places it in the category of Miami fiction. Hall is interested in dealing with the issue of a human being pushed into a situation where his life and values are seriously challenged, so his central character is an existentialist-loner called Thorn, a Hemingway figure who lives in a remote Key Largo stilt house and ties flies for a living. The novel's epigraph is from *A Writer's Journal* and Thorn tries to live according to the rhythms of nature, as Thoreau had done on the shores of Walden Pond. At the book's conclusion Thorn is purged of guilt and exorcizes the memory of killing his lover's father, whom he kidnappped from his home in leafy suburban Coral Gables, the setting for the violent conclusion of the text's thriller plot. Another type of floater, Thorn bathes in Lake Surprise, thus becoming himself, as Thoreau predicted, 'a still lake of purest crystal'.

Hiassen's forte is black humour: 'Sparky' Harper the President of the Greater Miami Chamber of Commerce is choked to death with a 79 cents rubber alligator – still displaying its price tag. The crusading terrorists are out to make a point: the body chopped off at the legs and dressed in a Jimmy Buffett shirt and Bermuda shorts is stuffed in a suitcase, the Royal Tourister ... Hiassen's later and more coherent novel *Double Whammy* (1987), whose title is the name of a lure for bass, is an exposé of fraud and murder among redneck fishermen in the Southeastern states, especially Florida. In this instance the environmentalist response to real estate development on the edge of the Everglades, where the state fish, the largemouth bass, is dangerously polluted, is divorced from the text's more imaginative Gothicisms. Thomas Curl, a foul-mouthed killer, is savaged by a pit bull terrier with a 'supernatural' grip. Unable to release from his arm the 'demonic mandibles' of the dog (dispatched by the thrust of a screwdriver), Curl severs the head still attached as though in symbiosis and continues his murderous journey. The symbolism – Curl's bestiality, the moral corruption made physical by infection – is crudely obvious, but is pursued with grim panache through the redneck's explosive death and a feast for buzzards who reduce the dog's head to a bare yellow skull.

Chucky in *Stick* once killed a dog and was moved out of Georgia because of his 'mental' problem. His diet of Valium and 'ludes causes him to float among the coloured lights in his head: the sensation of swimming under water – without the water. His own violence remains latent until the novel reaches its climax, but he belongs nevertheless to that company of psychopaths (Frenger in *Miami Blues*, Louden in Willeford's *Sideswipe*, Norodny in *Floater*, McMann in *Under Cover of Daylight*) which serves to activate the plot throughout the Miami/Florida intertext. The blankness of tone identified in *Miami Vice* (what Fredric Jameson

defining postmodernism calls waning of affect) is, in these characters, translated into abnormal psychology so that moral vacancy
replaces conscience. Committing one of his murders, Norodny has
'the disinterested gaze of a man preoccupied with other things as if
he might be expecting an important phone call'. For this unreachable
type killing is work, a business even: 'What I did I did to eat, to eat
well. It's not my hobby.' His self-image precludes guilt and re-
morse: 'I like kids, a day at the ball park. I pay my taxes on time.'[11]

   The alternative to floating Chucky-style is a kind of existen-
tialism achieved by establishing your identity, your personal style,
or by just playing a role. Performance anxiety is a pervasive feeling
in Leonard's novels. The exhibition is often based in language:
Latinos in *Stick* dress up, pose and throw out TV lines like 'What's
happening, man?' In *LaBrava*,as the eponymous photographer de-
risively observes, Richie Nobles's act is based upon a stereotype of
masculinity, specifically the all-American boy: 'Hometown boy –
the hair, the toothpick, the hint of swagger in the set of silver-clad
shoulders. What an asshole. How did they get so sure of themselves, these guys, without knowing anything? Like people who
have read one book.'[12] To Cundo Rey, the 'boatlifter' from a Cuban
prison and Nobles's partner in crime, his own style is more authentic; it is Nobles the Florida redneck, the swamp creature who is the
alien, Cundo the real American, the man of the city.

   In *Floater* Norodny uses a stolen plane ticket to Hollywood
(Florida); the textual narrative is Hitchcock's *Shadow of a Doubt*
re-made by Brian De Palma and ending with a car chase. It is in
Leonard's books however that role playing is most frequently associated with the cinema. Most of *Get Shorty* (1990) takes place in
Hollywood , the dream dump of Nathanael West acting once more
as a metaphor of America where dream becomes reality. (The
climax is played out to the accompaniment on tape of Marvin
Gaye's blues version of The Star Spangled Banner.) In an industry
where the bosses and workers are hardly able to differentiate between
cinema and life, where no one is in charge and there are no rules,
aesthetic or moral, it is logical that Chili Palmer, loan shark and
debt collector for the mob in Miami, should succeed as a co-
producer in Hollywood.

   Even Chili is immersed in film culture imagining himself at
4.30 in the morning in Robert De Niro roles. Meanwhile, down-
stairs, Chili's antagonist, drug pusher Bo Catlett, is listening to the
big gun battle in *Rio Bravo*, the fate of the villains falling through

those 'rickety porch railings' neatly prefiguring his own imminent death. Leonard even includes a reference to one of his own screenplays, that for the Clint Eastwood film *Joe Kidd*.

A fan of the glamorous movie star since the age of twelve, Joe LaBrava is blocked by desire and memory in his attempts to 'read' Jean Shaw with whom he is falling in love. Her image is made enigmatic by the star's ability to 'act her way out of a safe deposit box'. When most of her lines are from 1950s movies (in which she played Woman as Destroyer), LaBrava can only act along in the part provided for him, even at the novel's end uttering Jean Shaw's cynical closing line from countless B-movies: 'Swell'. Like the Spider Women she used to portray, Jean Shaw is 'disillusioned but knows she has to play the game'.[13] She is one of a number of smart, emotionally tough women in Leonard's recent novels such as Kathy Diaz Baker in *Maximum Bob* (1991), and Jackie Burke in *Rum Punch* (1992), women who are not averse to shooting homicidal criminals in defence of their husband or, in the case of Carmen Colson in the Detroit novel *Killshot*, to protect her home, which the part Ojibway hitman and robber Armand Degas has invaded.

The intertextuality in *LaBrava* is literary genre/film genre and, as in *Get Shorty*, book/movie. LaBrava wrenches his consciousness back to the present, persuading himself Jean Shaw is the victim in a 'real' drama. He misplaces the knowledge he has that the star has always played the same part, in this instance a member of a trio involved in an elaborate swindle. Leonard chooses to avoid generic determinism. The novel ends not with the *film noir* elimination of the *femme fatale*, but with her marriage to Maurice Zola whom she sought to dupe. In Miami, anything is possible.

The discourse of Leonard and other crime writers, especially the Miami school, is recalled and inflected in Richard Hoyt's *Marimba* (1992) – the title refers to the drug trade in Miami. Like *Miami Vice* it represents the law as a significant element in the perpetuation of drug traffic; like Hiassen's *Double Whammy* it inserts a savage voracious dog into the plot. A subplot involving the disappearance into Miami's seedy underworld of the younger sister of an FBI investigator (Katherine Donovan) recalls similar narrative strands in Ross Macdonald and Robert Parker.

Hoyt creates a quasi-symbiotic relationship between two players in the drug-dealing world, Guzmán, an ostentatiously affluent FBI agent turned cocaine trafficker; and his mirror image Burlane, apparently a wild, bohemian pilot/mercenary, in actuality working

on behalf of a government investigation. Through these and associated figures Hoyt maps the buildings and culture of glossy, stylish
Miami, from Burlane's South Miami apartment with its mustard
walls to Guzmán's deceptively modest white stucco Art Deco bun-
galow in Coral Gables which houses glass walls, Italian leather fur-
niture and $5000 originals painted by Mijares.

Food is central to the decoding of social and ethnic distinctions;
for Guzmán the ideal life of sex and drugs is preceded by rattlesnake
salad and buffalo sausage at Dominique's, but the food at El Pueblo's
with its range of ethnic specials accompanied by watermelon juice
bestows a sense of identity and pride. At the distant end of the food
spectrum, plastic buckets of fried chicken (Pollo Supreme) and stolen
champagne provide the fare in the scuzzy apartments where the
marginalised seek to survive.

The trajectory of pleasure and work takes in fashionable bars
(the News Café), Cuban mom-and-pop diners (El Pueblo), and
nightclubs such as Oysterman's, the scene of sexual and business
transactions made in an atmosphere where the spirit of display is
dominant. In the postmodern Miami of *Marimba* (and Leonard's
novels), appearance and performance are the key to acceptance and
success, as Guzmán's gold chains and diamond earring, and the (re-
movable) tattoos of coiled snakes decorating Katherine's cleavage,
testify.

Santería, the religion brought to the New World by African
slaves and to Florida by Cubans, connects *Marimba* with *The Killing of the Saints*. Like Ramón Valdez, Carmela Martinez, unusually for a santera or priestess, is given for her spirit, or *orisha*, the
fierce warrior Ogun, who urges her to prosper by means of the
cocaine trade. Ogun, Carmela and the white drug merge in a
monstrous triangular amalgamation.

Carmela, a Cuban immigrant and daughter of a secret police-
man for Batista, is also the matriarch of a united, pathological family of killers, including a sadistic, baseball-obsessed son and two
deadly, shopping-obsessed daughters, all in their own ways making
an accommodation with their culturally mixed inheritance. The voluptuous bodies of the Martinez women, adorned with designer
clothes, and those of the Miami Beach girls down from New York to
model covers for *Cosmopolitan* and *Vogue*, provide a sardonic contrast to the wasted, abused bodies of addicts such as the doomed
Helen Donovan. The most lethal member of the 'family' is the black
Doberman logically named Marimba who chews up human flesh

and blood. Similarly, the bodies of the next generation, symbolised by the naïve dog-loving child in the novel's final image, will be consumed as the *marimberos* continue to practice their trade inside a corrupt, decadent society. If Miami , as hyped by journalists, is the new frontier, the future will be as dark and brutal as the earlier frontiers of the American West.

NOTES

1   K. K. Rowe, 'Power in Prime Time: Miami Vice and L.A. Law', *Jump Cut* 33 (1988), 20.

2   E. Leonard, *Stick* (Harmondsworth, Penguin, 1984), pp. 82–3.

3   S. Zukin, *Landscapes of Power: From Detroit to Disney World* (Berkeley, University of California Press, 1991), p. 248.

4   R. Williams, *The Country and the City* (St. Albans, Paladin, 1975), p. 191.

5   Leonard, *Stick*, pp. 21, 120, 125.

6   Zukin, *Landscapes of Power*, pp. 244–5.

7   R. Sparks, *Television and the drama of crime: moral tales and the place of crime in public life* (Buckingham, Philadelphia, Open University Press, 1992), p.126.

8   C. Willeford, *Miami Blues* (New York, Ballantine, 1985), pp. 31, 143–4.

9   *Ibid*, p. 157.

10   B. Mukherjee, 'Loose Ends' in *The Middleman and other stories* (London,Virago, 1990), p. 48.

11   J. Koenig, *Floater* (Harmondsworth, Penguin, 1989), pp. 70, 273.

12   E. Leonard, *LaBrava* (Harmondsworth, Penguin,1985), p. 133.

13   *Ibid*, pp. 262, 183.

6

CINEMA AND THE
CITIES OF CRIME

Big city crime with its opportunities for pursuit and other physical action was a staple element in silent movies from their inception, establishing many of the patterns of the gangster film. In 1904 *The Capture of the Yegg Bank Burglar*, based on a book by William A. Pinkerton, indicated an early interest in the PI by East Coast film-makers. D. W. Griffith's *The Musketeers of Pig Alley* (1912) was a formative work in several ways: its documentary realism, its all too brief location work in the ghettos of New York, its introduction of an archetypal slum roughneck as swaggering racketeer (here the Snapper Kid), and finally, despite Griffith's Southern perception of the city as the focus of vice and corruption, the absence of moralising. Griffith, and his cameraman Billy Bitzer, created the atmosphere of the early twentieth century through images of tenement life and teeming street scenes of immigrants, beggars, hurdy-gurdy men, and the descendants of the urban 'bandits' photographed in the Mulberry Street area by Jacob Riis, whose exposé *How the Other Half Lives* had been published in 1890. However Griffith's city space in the film acts as both milieu and restraint with static interior shots that give a sense of claustrophobia.

'In the metropolis there is no longer pan-orama (the vision of all), because its body overflows beyond the horizon. In the metro-politan aesthetic the eye fails in its role as an instrument of total control at a distance; once more the ears, and then the nose and skin, acquire an equal importance. The sensory field of the metropolis is ultra-and infra-visual: it is the field of a total aesthetic'.[1] Mazzoleni's discussion of the problematic nature of experiencing the city leads us to sound cinema which once more foregrounds the auditory. The possibility of kinaesthetic moments is created by cinematic resources playing on concentration of feeling and on personal memory; the extravagant, sensuous display of flowers and food in rich New York interiors in Scorsese's *The Age of Innocence* (1993) offers a suitable example. The inside of a dark cinema resembles the metropolis itself, insofar as it is a habitat without a 'somewhere else'. Finally, Mazzoleni portrays the nature of metropolitan spatiality as 'the imaginary space of the mind' which suggests a further affiliation with the cinematic experience.

Early sound films in the 1930s registered physical changes in the city. The narrative of *Public Enemy* (1931) begins in 1909 showing the juxtaposition of horse-drawn vehicles, automobiles and trolley cars. More importantly it responds to a shift in perspective towards crime and the underclass. Earlier the silent movie, while eventually starting to come to terms with the ghetto, had often expressed the censorious views of the respectable Anglophone hegemony towards ethnic neighbourhoods which were regarded as the sites of debauchery. Following the economic and social upheavals of the Wall Street crash and its aftermath, WASP culture experienced a legitimation crisis. The simple moralism of the old urban narratives had become outmoded and cultural boundaries were being called into question. Ethnic experience and the gangster were allowed verbal and visual expression through the vernacular voices and body gestures of Cagney and Robinson. Nationalised city noises, the polyphony of street talk, and the use of representational space to show the increased impact of the underworld marked the appearance of a new, subversive USA.

The skyscraper, a popular motif in advertising and fashion, had by the 1920s become an essential constituent of urban films and, especially in its Art Deco form, a symbol of Manhattan. The emphasis on verticality implied a transcendence of the noise and congestion of the streets. This period of celebratory, romantic realism saw the rise of the 'city symphony' style, notably in artistic documentaries such as Paul Strand's optimistic, modernist presentation of the aesthetic city *Mannahatta* (1921), and Robert Flaherty's lyrically abstract *24 Dollar Island* (1925). In the commercial cinema of the 1930s the emphasis was on monumentality, dynamism and spatial relations, with the dynamism extending to the rhythm of dancing skyscrapers ....

The film version of *Dead End* (1937) reproduced the class divisions of Lang's skyscraper city in *Metropolis*. Beginning with the panoramic, studio-built skyline of the city, the camera moves downwards from the towers of the rich to the waterfront, a crime school for tenement urchins. Later, in the 1940s and 1950s, when the theme of the corrupt city dominated crime films, skyscrapers became perceived as the common territory of mafiosi, dubious politicos and shyster lawyers. Their ominous power renders the canyons of concrete and steel overwhelming at street level. The juxtaposition of giant building and dwarfed, anonymous individual became a standard visual device in both film and photography, and was used in the postwar decades to depict, through modernist architecture, the oppressive power of corporate capitalism.

In this negative representation the skyscraper is associated with banks, offices and Wall Street. The high angle shots at the start of *Force of Evil* (1948) depict the overbearing slabs of Wall Street which appear to threaten Lower Manhattan's ancient Trinity Church. Juxtaposed with the world of Wall Street lawyers is the contrasting neighbourhood community of the protagonist's brother, a friendly small-time numbers operator doomed to 'disappear' by leading racketeers. His body is left at the foot of the George Washington Bridge whose monumental steps stretch down, in the words of Leo's brother, 'to the bottom of the world'. Later in *Tight Spot* (1955) a stool pigeon taken from Staten Island to testify against the Mafia is shot outside a courthouse in Lower Manhattan, whereupon his guards turn to confront the windows of Wall Street.

In the Thirties and Forties, Hollywood sets became the urban background for mobster narratives and *film noir* texts, supporting the adverse view of the city as alien and immoral that recurs throughout American history. In the hard-boiled fiction of the 1920s and the Depression, the 'otherness' of Afro-Americans, immigrants (especially Chinese) and women makes them strange and threatening. *Film noir* interprets male criminals and women as outsiders, though the sense of dispossession is general, and duplicitous women are not solely to be blamed for the anxiety which pervades the entire milieu.

Particular locales, charged with tension and mystery, are selected which collectively signify 'city': rain-soaked streets, bars, warehouses, penthouses, and especially night clubs epitomising the dream-like, flaky glamour of the 1940s, whether in New York (*Phantom Lady*) or Buenos Aires (*Gilda*). In *Road House* (1948) the night club in the rural small town (its only hotel is *The Antlers*) provides the stage for a triangular drama of lust, violence and, in Jeffty the club owner (Richard Widmark), sadistic possessiveness. Jeffty with his sharp suit and hat is a familiar urban type, malicious and potentially unstable. Lily, the new torch singer from Chicago, enlivens the town and initiates the narrative. Glamorous and sophisticated, she acknowledges opera on the radio during a confidential tête-a-tête with the club manager Pete. However Lily lacks the duplicity characteristic of the sexy, urban adventuress and, available for domestication, she finds her love for Pete threatened only by the manic Jeffty who ends up literally hunting them down in the neighbouring woods.

The technology of guns, automobiles and telephones supplements these expressionist extensions of a brutal world. Office blocks show the increasing size of corporations and the growth of monopolies. As small businesses are squeezed, middle class staff join the lonely crowd working for big organisations like Pacific All Risk Insurance in Wilder's *Double Indemnity*. A typical example of urban imagery in this genre is *Street With No Name* (1948) which moves between bus depots, penny arcades, pool halls and cheap boarding houses, to the accompaniment of a jazz soundtrack. *Film noir* angst emanates from the principal gangster played by Richard Widmark, his psychosis marked this time by an obsession with his nasal spray and the intrusion of fresh air.

The city in *film noir* becomes the site of paranoia and despair, conveyed by hysterical acting and by visual style, especially stylistic distortions. The protagonist adopts a fatalistic attitude because 'the city will outlast and negate even his best efforts. No character can speak authoritatively from a space which is being continually cut into ribbons of light.'[2] Non-naturalistic lighting and framing establishes an unsteady world of moral relativism in which all characters are subject to stylistic disruptions. Identities and values are constantly shifting.

Thus the behaviour of women, criminals and even detectives (the noir or 'black' figures as defined by a moralistic culture) is pronounced as shady since the opposition between good and bad, light and dark, is blurred. The collapse of boundaries may lead to an uncertainty or ambiguity of response on the part of the audience. More often the revelation of wickedness is deferred by plot details or deceptive visual presentation: in *Out of the Past*, Kathy, the duplicitous dark woman, first appears in a dream-like sequence as a shimmering white-clad image.

Style is at the centre of *film noir* in the sense of not only *mise-en-scène* but also fashion – in lighting, interiors (mirrors, lamps, curtains) and, in films like *Road House*, wisecracking language and clothes. By the 1950s *Kiss Me Deadly* (1955) with its neo-stream-lining, draughtboard floors and hi-fi system would adumbrate the bright gloss and consumerism of the 1960s. Private homes also functioned as encoded signs in crime movies of the 1940s, especially beach houses (in Malibu) and labyrinthine ranch houses. The latter, in Spanish Colonial Revival style with terraces and laurel shrub-bery, were often situated in Bel Air or Beverly Hills, the fictional territory of Chandler and Cain. It is the cinematic style of Cornell Woolrich which makes him a more immediate literary harbinger of *film noir*.

Woolrich is an anatomist of New York as the essential *film noir* city: 'the midnight streets, furnished rooms, low bars, dance halls, precinct offices, rain, heat, shadows, whiskey fumes and cigarette smoke'. In Woolrich's novels, New York at night is perceived as actively, monstrously malevolent, but it is a perception which releases paranoia: while the characters in *Deadline at Dawn* (1946) move through 'a defamiliarized, maze-like nocturnal landscape', that landscape resembles 'a massive, monolithic sepulchre'.³ The city, with its empty lots and warehouses without windows, appears empty and lifeless.

The first half of *Phantom Lady* (1944) directed in expressionist style by emigré Robert Siodmak and based on Woolrich's novel, focuses on the constructed nature of the *femme fatale*. With her boss Henderson accused of murder, 'Kansas' (Ella Raines) an intelli-gent, enterprising professional in his engineering company, achieves the identity of 'dark lady' by means of sexy clothes and bright make-up. Her quest takes her into the infernal regions of a jazz cel-lar, the air tinged with booze and filled with reefer smoke and the sound of bebop rhythms. Her mask-like face, a standard image in *film noir* and in Joan Crawford melodramas, is the frozen tablet on which the hapless male, here the bartender, inscribes not his desires in this instance but his fears. Pursued by Kansas through wet New York streets to the El – she is both temptress and detective – he panics and is hit by an automobile.

Ted Tetzlaff's *The Window* (1949) is attentive to working-class life in the Lower East Side through such images as laundry strung between buildings, reminiscent of Ash Can illustrations like John Sloan's 1910 etching 'Night Windows'. The characteristically op-pressive atmosphere of New York is once more captured by orches-trated details: abandoned buildings, grime and dust, the noise of the

El, and a heatwave which forces the central character Tommy to sleep on the fire escape thus triggering the plot. The theme is evident from the original Woolrich tale, 'The Boy Who Cried Wolf'. Tommy has to endure a nightmarish and futile journey through the city's dangerous streets followed, at the film's end, by a tense flight from his murderous neighbour. The derelict building where he also sleeps and dreams is the scene of their final confrontation. Its collapse kills the neighbour and threatens Tommy but hints at the larger significance of urban renewal and suburbanisation : 'film noir registered [the] decline [of the metropolis], accomplishing a demonization and an estrangement from its landscape in advance of its actual "abandonment" '.[4]

The New York film most often cited for its role in the history of postwar Hollywood is *The Naked City* (1948), made on location in semi-documentary style. The weary voiceover which matches the exhaustion of the New Yorkers condemned to the daily grind and noisy, disturbed nights recalls *film noir* where it was a staple technique; nevertheless the film is a visual 'police procedural' glorifying the dull, routine work of investigating detectives.

The movie title was bought from the New York photographer Weegee (it belongs equally to his best known portfolio *Naked City*, published in 1945). The association is meaningful: Weegee's intrusive, transgressive camera designed a nocturnal, dramatic world of criminals by means of a work routine that shadowed the forces of law. He had his own police radio. For miscreants the frustration of arrest was augmented by the shame of indentification through Weegee's flash photography. His morbid trespassing was matched by the activity of Dassin's documentary camera hidden in phone boxes and fake ambulances, a further example of the vulnerability of the urban crowd to spying and surveillance.

New York congestion enables the murderer in Dassin's film to mingle and avoid detection. As in Joe Gores's San Francisco novel, *Gone, No Forwarding*, the city's 'eight million people struggling for life, for food, for air, for a bit of happiness' are statistics, their lives as numerical as squad cars or precincts. Events and destinies are at the mercy of chance. The task of the police is to rationalise the random, to evacuate the geographical space between separate crime scenes (here Queens and the East Side) by establishing a relationship.

The authentic New York police procedural film, rough and gritty, was carried to another level with *The French Connection*

(1971) which employed 86 city locations for its real life narrative of drug trafficking between Marseilles and New York. While it exhibits the endeavours of the Police Department on the streets and has a sound track that combines vernacular speech with painful, debilitating noise, the film, coolly detached in its moral and emotional stance, tends towards the abstract. This is apparent in its perceptions of cars which pushes the film closer to an LA style: 'There are loving close-shots of license plates and bumper lights, dizzying viewpoint shots from cars in motion, zooms through the windshield, quietly intense takes of cars stalking other cars through night streets.'[5]

The vision *The French Connection* constructs is typically that of the crisis-torn, decaying city where the most identifiable and widespread emotion is a near-hysterical anxiety. Pauline Kael, reviewing the movie in *Deeper Into Movies* (1975), records the growing incidence of 'fights and semi-psychotic episodes' when brutal, suspenseful films (often set in New York) were playing in Times Square and the Village. The assertive rawness and cynical realism of *The French Connection* crystallise in the characterisation of the central figure 'Popeye' Doyle, a fast-food guzzling and racist cop, as lawless and sadistic as the dealers he hunts, and more vulgar and scurrilous in his colloquial speech than the suave French drug runners who take elegant meals at Copain on First Avenue.

The geographical and social spectrum of Manhattan runs from First Avenue, with its smart restaurants, to Ward's Island, the no-man's land which serves as the culmination of the film's sequence of urban images: tenements, junkyards, graffiti, old bridges and used car lots. Best known for its toxic waste dumps and hospital for the criminally insane, Ward's Island, one of the desolate settings in Andrew Vachss' *Hard Candy*, also houses a school for garbagemen, among them the brother of Salvatore Boca, a small-time dealer tracked by Popeye. In the film's climax Sal dies on a pile of cardboard boxes, part of the detritus which, along with stark, wintry trees, forms the landscape of Ward's Island. In the semi-abstract denouement, Popeye still pursuing 'Frog One' through a burnt-out factory, walks away from the camera as though sucked into the gloom, to the puzzling accompaniment of a gunshot. The crime text like the city itself resists the oversimplification of conclusive action.

The naturalism of *The French Connection* is overlaid with colour and decor in Martin Scorsese's *Mean Streets* (1973) and *Taxi Driver* (1976) which, in their shared image of the violent city, pay tribute to the New York films of the 1940s. The title of the former refers to the famous Chandler quotation: 'Down these mean streets a man must go who is not himself mean . . . ', and receives an echo in Michael's concern with his dignity, threatened by Johnny Boy's irrationality and refusal to pay his debts. The film's referentiality however is visual, including clips from old films (notably the crime classic *The Big Heat*) as well as photographs and home movies. The exuberant hand-held camera, unusual examples of *mise-en-scène* and the use of slow motion are constituents of an expressionistic style, best observed in Tony's bar where an embracing darkness, pierced by a lurid miasma of red, surrounds the poses, emotions, gestures and physicality of a group of young rowdies in New York's Little Italy.

The active centre of Tony's bar is a jukebox which pumps pop music into the atmosphere turning it into the medium for the guys' everyday experience. Like the music, their street language is staccato, brusque and intense. The chatter of male friendship (Scorsese's New York is largely a man's world), is also tentative – the interrogative mode either a worried deferral, or a badass challenge; Johnny Boy's 'You talkin' to me?'(practised by Travis in *Taxi Driver*) is a variation of the standard 'mind fucking' question recorded by social anthropologists, 'Whachoolookinat?' The group's rhythmic street rhetoric with its litany of insulting names – scumbag, jerkoff, mook (moocher or tightwad) – becomes a resource for adolescent time-filling and posturing. There is an understood repertoire of rhythms and vocabulary but far from being liberating, the vernacular is part of the desperate struggle for connections.

The music is mainly urban soul, interspersed with Motown, Rolling Stones, R and B, and doo wop, an eclectic mix ranging from lyrical anthems to rabble-rousers like Johnny's entrance number, 'Jumpin' Jack Flash'. It is the sound of a discontinuous culture in which satisfactions are shortlived. 'The culture of *Mean Streets* operates at a molecular level of collision, speed, exorbitance, severe shudders of perspective ... Pleasure for the adolescents carries with it the pledge of disaster and neither youth nor ethnic culture can bind them together.'[6]

Michael, a loan shark, imports unlicensed foreign goods, and the criminality of the young Italian-Americans is limited to wheeling and dealing. Although they live in a milieu of crime, the mean streets of New York (the low budget movie was mainly shot in LA) are essentially a stage for random performances which involve arguing, sparring and brawling. Suspicious and ritualistic, the gang resembles the Mafia, epitomised by the godfather figure of Charlie's powerful uncle Giovanni, to whom they are linked by blood. Charlie and Michael wear the long tailored overcoats that signify organised crime.

The insularity of the members of the subcultural group is shown in a further way. Their appropriation of urban soul music is part of an ambivalent response to the adjacent black world which, like the culture of Jews or gays, remains unknowably 'other' and separate. Inside the narrow geographical boundaries of the community, their own ethnic identity is fragile, with the exception of Charlie who is given the personality of a tormented guilt-ridden priest, seeking redemption and justification in a fallen world. Religion has been displaced by pop music making ironic the traditional brass band's parade at the Feast of St Gennaro. Distanced from the certainties of the past enjoyed by older generations, the young men rely on pro-visional codes of taste and style which influence their appearance and gestures.

In this frenzied populist opera of a wiseguy culture running adrift, Johnny Boy (Robert De Niro) expresses the film's most bale-ful meanings. One shot aims the gun in the poster advertising *Point Blank* towards his head, and from his first literally explosive entrance he dances deliriously towards punishment and doom. The counter-part to the music's volatility and turbulence, Johnny evokes the psychotic, suicidal last phase of classic *film noir*, while also emerg-ing as a cinematic equivalent to the unstable, atavistic psychopaths of hard-boiled fiction in the 1980s.

In his insularity and psychosis, and in the way he switches between disconnected parts of his personality, Travis Bickle (De Niro once more) in *Taxi Driver* is a later version of Johnny Boy; one in which the emptiness is more palpable because no group of small-time hoods is available for joshing and scrapping. It is the move-ments of the hopped-up street pimp Sport (Harvey Keitel), wiggling and gesticulating as he taunts Bickle, and the malign rhetoric of the gun salesman (Steven Prince) which evoke more readily Johnny's physical and verbal displays in *Mean Streets*.

The New York of *Taxi Driver* turns restless although the alien-ated Travis moves towards a numbness, a growing repression that ultimately bursts into ferocious, massive violence. Haunted by its filth and brutality Travis hates the city; his hatred becomes an ob-session which he feeds at night by driving a taxi-cab on the back seat of which his customers leave blood and semen. His (and Scorsese's) New York is the City of Dreadful Night, squalid and viscous yet also trance-like and sensual. Travis, who will drive to any part of the city including Harlem and the Bronx, is thus absorbed by the environment yet remains remote from it. Staring at other people he is part spy, attempting to make sense of the spectacle of the city. He is also a type of suffering anti-*flâneur*, unable to discover and relish pleasure, to 'live it up' as the ad on a cross-town bus urges.

Travis's misery is the product of his psychology (paranoia, inability to communicate) and his isolated urban condition in an infernal New York, a 'sweltering night city of shadows, neon lights, shimmering shapes and manhole covers emitting steam'.[7] He longs for an event of biblical proportions, a cleansing storm that will 'wash away all the scum off the streets'. Travis himself takes on this mission plunging into the urban jungle he despised earlier, his Mohawk haircut the sign of his asceticism as well as the idealised purity of lakes and forests. It also anticipates a later De Niro film, *The Deerhunter* (1978), in which the preoccupation with Vietnam would be predominant. Previously his grubby rented room was a cell within the larger open prison of the metropolis, yet with sufficient space for his aberrant perceptions. The psychosis obscured in other avengers (notably Clint Eastwood's Callahan in *Dirty Harry*, 1971) is here brought to the surface and Travis crosses his own frontier to enact a bloodbath in a brothel. A warrior once more, the Vietnam vet turns New York into Saigon.

Scorsese's 'Expressionist' vision of New York presses an hallucinatory style and the dark ambience of *film noir* upon the kind of documentary locations familiar from other examples of the city/ crime film, evoked through a yearning sax on the soundtrack. 'The street vapors become ghostly; Sport the pimp romancing his baby whore leads her in an hypnotic dance; the porno theatres are like mortuaries; the congested traffic is macabre.'[8] The film's screenwriter, Paul Schrader, called the taxi a metal coffin and a symbol of urban loneliness. For Travis it is another claustrophobic jail from which he witnesses muggings and rough sexual episodes, forms of violence in which he will ultimately partake. The familiar yellow New York cab is a crucial ingredient of the cinematographer's palette used with smoke, tinting and dissolves in the opening dislocating shots which might have strayed from a science fiction movie. Later its looming presence as it drifts through the distorted but vibrating streets helps to establish the movie's ominous, unsettling mood.

Taxi Driver is not a social realist's account of rancid urban decay; instead the excremental city becomes an aesthetic object both appalling and fascinating. Scorsese's self-conscious direction (voice-over, close-ups, slow motion) acknowledges and inflects the genre of the big city thriller with motifs of horror and grim humour. Travis, drinking, popping pills and going to porno movies, is himself part of the dispossessed underworld of pimps, whores and marginal types that he despises; temperamentally and as part of his job he circulates inside the city like them. The film's final irony lies in Travis's reception by the press and others as a moral hero. For him, as for Flitcraft in Sam Spade's parable, the beams seem to have stopped falling, and he is observed in front of the St Regis picking up passengers again. Travis's haunted eyes stay reflected in the rear view mirror: for him, the city has been an interior space which the perceiving subject has attempted to map in order to find his place within it. The wild carnage in the brothel can be traced to the failures and frustrations of that quest.

In their conception of the city, later 'noir' films of the 1960s and 1970s (*Point Blank* (1967); *The Long Goodbye* (1973)) prepare the way for the delirious, mannered metropolis of films like *Batman Returns*. The cinematic city of this period, formalistic in decor and architecture, is more a work of graphic art than an environment to inhabit, so that place generates plot action but no longer correlates to an aspect of the characters' inner lives .

Instead of reflecting character, landscape impinges on the protagonist and visibly contributes to his alienation. The baffling world of *film noir* is now discontinuous, a condition suffered by the 'hero', who finds the spatial setting separated (by, for example, Godard's montage in *Alphaville* (1965) from his personal narration. The result is two types of emptiness: 'an environment stylized towards the future with a spurious notion of progress, and a figure oriented in equally formal terms to the past'.[9] The representation of the desolate artificial city is powerful and evocative, but such achievements are reached at the cost of failing to establish personal identity.

Violence, often emanating from the hero's frustrated estrangement, becomes grotesque even funny, as in the later clutch of cartoon-inspired movies from *Who Framed Roger Rabbit* to *The Mask*. The violence cannot alter the city whose formalism demands either acceptance or (in *Alphaville*) escape. Crime now becomes co-existent with the status quo; all institutions adopt the structure of the amoral underworld. *Film noir* of the 1940s explored moral decline but in its successors moral enquiry is no longer appropriate.

The narrative of John Boorman's film *Point Blank* – and the original novel by Richard Stark (Donald E. Westlake) – is a quest for money and justice. The hunter who seeks to penetrate the bureaucratic maze of mobster businessmen (and whose existential search necessitates an exploration of the modern city) is himself a criminal. Paradoxically he is like the PI of hard-boiled fiction, uniquely honorable and resilient. The reality he confronts in *Point Blank* resists analysis and the hallucinatory, incomprehensible metropolis renders him bewildered and confused; 'chasing shadows' he becomes vulnerable to betrayal and sudden extinction.

Specific Los Angeles locations are shown – the LA River, Hollywood Hills, the city freeways – but Walker's investigations, increasingly undertaken in a spirit of disgust, anatomise the city as a collection of spaces and interiors relevant to the operation of the syndicate: nightclub, used car lot, penthouse, sewer system. Both the neon-lit corridors of corporate tower buildings and the cold grey and silver of his ex-wife's apartment are instances of atmospheric urban design in 'late noir', dehumanised and moribund. The cynical culture of the syndicate (public) and the private 'domestic' scenes represented are mutually reflective; the tycoon's expensive house in the hills with its panoramic view of LA is bare and uninhabited. All its life is in its electrical kitchen equipment.

Point Blank begins and ends elsewhere: in San Francisco's prison on Alcatraz Island where Walker at the film's opening is left to die. Here too there is an emptiness and a feeling of abandonment. By the conclusion the empty cells are displaced as focus by the courtyard where half-lit arches and cloisters resemble underground catacombs conceived by, for example, Piranesi. In this ritualistic setting, a residue of Hammett's San Francisco Gothicism, Walker who simply disappears, or dies, is told his money is as 'safe as a church'.

Earlier, the LA River with its surrounding fences and brilliant white concrete also suggests a prison, becoming an emblem for human futility as characters slide uncontrollably down the slopes to provide sitting targets. It is in these abstract scenes, at and around the storm drain, the urban equivalent of a desert, that the formalised images of cityscape, huge concrete lattices, freeway viaducts, pipes and pylons are the most actively menacing and oppressive.

Although the LA River is a damp river bed, a minor character is dumped there to drown in Polanski's *Chinatown* (1974). Water and conspiracy suffuse the film. A spokesman for the proposed Alto Vallejo dam delivers a cautionary speech with biblical overtones: 'We live next door to the ocean, but we also live on the edge of the desert. LA is a desert community. Beneath this building, beneath our streets is a desert and without water the dust will rise up and cover us as though we never existed.' The dam to irrigate the surrounding land turns out to be a confidence trick. The City Water Commission's chief engineer Hollis Mulwray (a pun on the name of Mulholland who masterminded the LA system of aqueducts) refuses to build it and is killed in his own pond, the lilies providing emblems of death and decay. As the ex-cop and PI J. J. Gittes, employed to investigate alleged infidelity by Mulwray and subsequently his murder, travels through LA he penetrates the social and geopolitical system of the city, but uncovers a depravity and an acquiescent attitude to wickedness which defeats him.

Made at the time of the Watergate revelations but set in the 1930s, *Chinatown* is an enigmatic *film noir*, whose plot is based on the city's own history of scandals involving water rights and real estate scams. The drought is manufactured by Noah Cross who plans to divert water away from LA to the North West Valley where he has secretly bought up land. Cross, a creature of immense malevolence whose daughter Evelyn is married to Mulwray, is at the centre of this narrative of public and private perversity. In the blunt words of Robert Towne who wrote the screenplay, he is 'a man who raped the land and his own daughter'. Earlier in the film Evelyn is visualised as the movie's Spiderwoman: long fingernails, tailored suits, brittle make-up which also at times renders her as Oriental, and a self-possessed but evasive manner symbolised by her half-veiled hats. Her history re-positions her as innocent victim of incest, and Gittes's investigation ensures that, as in a previous case, his efforts to protect her are futile and disastrous.

The preceding failure occurred in Chinatown towards which the narrative is impelled by references, Chinese images and the appearances of Chinese servants. Only in the final scene does Chinatown, with its history of gambling rooms, opium dens and tong wars in the 1920s, become a place. Until then it remains a sign of Orientalism, mystery and otherness, an enigmatic signifier representing the unfathomable. As Gittes says, 'You can't always tell what's going on there.'

The cliché of the inexplicable and, in the Anglo puritan imagination, immoral Oriental is also historically an alibi for the dispossession of immigrants ghettoised to face poverty and internal exile. Gittes reveals that in Chinatown police practice was to 'look the other way'. It is into the trap laid by his old Chinatown partner, Lieutenant Escobar, that Gittes inadvertently lures Evelyn and her daughter Caroline. Cross's double violation remains unpunished and he is last seen hustling the vulnerable Caroline away from the scene. First silenced and handcuffed and then, following Evelyn's death, isolated and demoralised, Gittes wanders off into the neighbourhood's dark heart. LA's Chinatown echoes its San Francisco equivalent as an urban site of social pathology; in 'Dead Yellow Women' the Continental Op admits, 'If I never have to visit Chinatown again it'll be soon enough.'

Peter Wollen has claimed that 'the great films of the twentieth century are often, paradoxically, studio-made films, triumphs of design rather than realistic photographic renderings of the mean streets themselves'. His opposition of cinema and skyscraper on technical grounds (tracking shot versus elevator) is bizarre, though in *Blade Runner* for instance, camera technique needs the assistance of models and illusion to produce vertiginous moments of vertical spatiality. A further argument of Wollen's provides an echo of Mazzoleni's 'imaginary': 'the city is perceived as a kind of dream space, a delirious world of psychic projection rather than sociological delineation', satisfying unconscious desires, fears and fantasies.[10]

Sometimes the benefits that come from shooting in the studio are simply a lucky break. Wenders' *Hammett*, now a cult movie in film schools, was originally filmed on the streets of San Francisco, in City Hall and on the old ferryboats tied up at the Hyde Street pier; the released version with its artificially created smoky brown atmosphere was made on the studio lot in Los Angeles, and dispensed with most of the San Francisco footage. In contrast, *The Window* used real New York locations in a non-naturalistic way such as to give the impression of a studio-bound set, the kind used in early *film noir* to produce gaunt, semi-abstract cityscapes. After the war the fashion for location shooting in a documentary style became standard for city films. What was gained by embracing the circulations of urban life was offset by a diminution of evocation, of expressionist poetry.

Influenced by *film noir*, contemporary examples of the city film (*Blade Runner, Batman Returns, Who Framed Roger Rabbit*) recapture that poetry. They articulate dark nightmares from the world of graphic novels such as *Watchmen* rather than dreams, and find their appropriate style in Surrealism and Expressionism. Thus the stylised world created on film is a postmodern version of the Modernists' Unreal City, a post-Fordist city of deindustrialisation, sharp economic divisions, ethnic mingling and small scale entrepreneurship in local markets. Like the world of *film noir*, it is a chaotic dangerous milieu, whose representation, Wollen concludes, demands melodrama and the grotesque rather than the rationality of 'realism'.

Ridley Scott's *Blade Runner* (1982), based on a science-fiction novel by Philip K. Dick is set in the Los Angeles of 2019, a decrepit megalopolis in a state of post-industrial decay, a dystopia nicknamed 'Scott's Inferno' during shooting. 'Empty warehouses and abandoned industrial plant drip with leaking [acid] rain. Mist swirls, rubbish piles up, infrastructures are in a state of disintegration ... Punks and scavengers roam among the garbage ... ' Elsewhere, in and above the city, blazes a high-tech world of flying machines, videoscreens and skyscrapers dominated by the gargantuan building of the Tyrell organisation, a symbol of huge corporate power which monitors the activities on the ground. Yet this futuristic denial of LA's preferred image of cubic houses, beaches, sunshine and bright blue swimming pools, publicised by the paintings of David Hockney, is paradoxically close in spirit to the contemporary photographs of Robert Morrow in *City of Quartz*.

The Tyrell building which looks like an Egyptian pyramid or Mayan temple owes something to the neo-Mayan designs of LA visionaries Robert Stacy-Judd and Francisco Mujica in the 1920s. A more recent model is the College Life Insurance Company of America building (Roche, Dinkaloo and Associates, 1972) near Indianapolis, while its external lifts recall the Bonaventure Hotel in LA, a focus of postmodern debate. The 97th floor apartment of Deckard the bounty hunter/protagonist, where the Mayan influence is also evident, resembles Frank Lloyd Wright in his Charles Ennis House phase. Indeed, 'the chaos of signs, of competing significations and messages, suggests a condition of fragmentation and uncertainty at street level that emphasizes ... postmodern aesthetics ... '[11] This postmodern pastiching includes Chinese neon dragons as well as Graeco-Roman columns.

The contemporary architecture seems fastened upon the old, but the past keeps showing through, as with the empty space of the old Bradbury Building (1893) in downtown LA on the grillwork of whose cast-iron balconies and stairways the camera lingers. To underline the visual confusion of periods here, it should be pointed out that the building was inspired by a description in Edward Bellamy's utopian fiction *Looking Backward* (1887) which sends its time traveller to Boston in the year 2000. Its sole human inhabitant in the film, the young but wrinkled genetic designer J. F. Sebastian, is in a condition of 'accelerated decrepitude', supplying a perfect image of the city itself.

Street life is a visualisation and extension of David Rieff's title, *Los Angeles: Capital of the Third World*. Thoroughfares where bicycles have replaced automobiles in what was America's most motorised city swarm with a variety of ethnic immigrants, an extrapolation from the LA of the 1990s with its Vietnamese shops, its modernised Little Tokyo and its huge Koreatown. *Blade Runner's* Orientals form an underground network, whether wheeling and dealing in the black market or engaged in cheap labour practices that involve low technology workshops and subcontracting. Noodle bars and craft stalls are demonstrations of individual enterprise in a materialistic city with no sense of community or tradition. The general impression, encouraged by the pervasive dampness and darkness and by a style which blocks direct perception, is one of claustrophobia though space is evident elsewhere in the city. Even out of doors the combination of dark skies, walls, clogged alleys and close-ups conveys the enclosure of urban space. Only in the dusty air of Tyrell's penthouse is sunlight able to penetrate.

The Los Angeles of *Blade Runner* is Chinatown as postindustrial market, used as background for Deckard's urban adventures. The film fails therefore to register 'the presence, probably epochal, of an enlarged low-wage working class, living and working in the central city, and creating its own spatialized social world: networks of recreation, piety, reproduction, and, ultimately, struggle'.[12] The separation of the business towers from street life give no sense of any tension between global capital and international labour in downtown Los Angeles.

The narrative events in the mysterious brooding city take place at night; lighting and characters are shadowy; among the visual signs are venetian blinds, mirrors and ceiling fans. Patently, *Blade Runner* is a pastiche of *film noir*. Deckard, who in the studio cut provides the voiceover, is a grouchy, hard-boiled detective in a trench coat, while Rachael, the replicant, who begins the film as Tyrell's assistant, is a sophisticated *femme fatale*, her 1940s provenance signified by lip gloss, period hair and masculine suits. Fashion in the movie is more often arrived at in bricolage style, mixing consumerism and recycling with assistance, it would appear, from the junk-store. On the street can be found the traditional bit players of *film noir* – dubious cops and small-time hoods – and *Blade Runner's* references are not only to futuristic city films but also to hard-boiled thrillers like *The Big Sleep*. Deckard is a composite of PI characteristics, a professional with no family, few friends, and a stoic ability to take physical punishment. Lacking the idealism of Marlowe his response to the oppression of the replicants is, in the studio cut, to flee to the unpolluted forests and mountains of the north with Rachael.

Blade Runner recalls *Chinatown* in its systematic eye and sight imagery. At the public level surveillance is carried out by paramilitary police (in hovercars which provide a panoramic view of the city), computers and even traffic lights. The visual depiction of government exhortations and advertisements for Pan Am and Coca-Cola is almost identical; government and corporate business are indistinguishable. These neon messages and the probings of searchlights are part of the city's intrusiveness, daily irritants which the rich in their towers can largely evade.

The longest running Batman comic has been 'Detective', and like *Blade Runner, Batman Returns* is a crime-fighting narrative saturated by a dark, stylised urban vision and dependent on antecedent representations. Burton's earlier cinematic exploration of the theme and character, *Batman* (1989) with its vast urban designs bathed in neon and steam made Gotham City into a 1980s version of *Metropolis* which was also inspired by the city of New York. The film's locations, Wayne Mansion, the chemical plant and especially the cathedral and its gargoyles, are linked by references to the Gothic. In general *Batman* is prolific in its referentiality whether to old Hollywood movies, the Dracula legend or comic books; visual signs and their manipulation are at the heart of the conflict between Batman and the Joker, the one retrieving images from the past, the other 'mutilating' them, though over-painting flops as a joke since it is an acknowledged avantgarde technique.

In the appropriate comics – and later, graphic novels – Gotham City is perceived as a dark wasteland, a distillation of the characteristics of the Lower East Side, Bedford Stuyvesant and the South Bronx. In the drawings deserted warehouses, garbage-filled alleys, abandoned building sites and lonely, deserted streets are overshadowed by menacing skyscrapers. As social criticism though the visual/verbal text is severely limited.

> Gotham is largely removed from a socio-economic context. The narratives deal with the crime rate, but not the unemployment rate; they deal with criminal brutality, but not brutalizing landlords; they deal with the greed of petty theft, but not poverty and hopelessness – in short, they deal with the transgressions of the underclasses but not the conditions that give rise to these transgressions.[13]

The graphic novel *The Dark Knight Returns* (1986) at least problematises Batman's role within a degenerate society. Traditionally he acted as guardian of the city fulfilling the state's repressive authoritarian role. Now in Frank Miller's text, turned into a middle-aged outlaw by the police force and the media, and aligned with a vigilante underclass, he is pursued on Reagan's orders by Superman, whom he accuses of being a government lackey and, measured by superhero standards, a joke. Batman still manages to achieve a Marlowe-like integrity, clinging to honour and striving for justice. Journeying on horseback to his climactic duel with the caped crusader, he retains his fabulous, legendary status.

The mocking laughter of the Joker in *Batman* expresses a motiveless evil which is hostile to the whole idea of value and significance. In *Batman Returns* city politics with contemporary implications assume prominence through the PR-led mayoral campaign (logos, posters, the media) and its accompanying rhetoric. But as the troubled Mayor is in the process of denouncing 'urban chaos' and the splintering of the community, a member of the Red Triangle Gang followed by Cobblepot (the Penguin) appears from subterranean drains. The effect of the invasion of Gotham City by a penguin army from the sewers (mentioned in the New York Chapter) is of a plague spreading steadily across the city.

Any suggestion that the Penguin and his followers are sympathetic in their pathos fails to take note of Cobblepot's infamous project to kill every first born son in the city. The struggle for space and power, taking place behind masked balls and the celebration of symbolic animals, displaces class conflict; the city becomes a theatre for the working out of destructive relationships. In the moral economy of *Batman Returns* the circus performers with their larky violence are demonised, an understandable demystification of sentimental infantilism, but a calamitous failure to realise the radical, carnivalesque potential of their outsider status.

The vertical space of the modern (or now postmodern) city is also a class space, with a rebellious underclass literally living underground, emerging from time to time to riot and bring terror to the aboveground citizenry, while the future of the city is plotted to their own crooked advantage by tycoons and politicians in skyscraper penthouses.[14] The removal of Batman himself from the centre serves the same purpose. No longer the rebellious outlaw of *The Dark Knight Returns* he is vulnerable to the machinations of Cobblepot and Shreck. In addition he responds uncertainly to the manifestations of power through sexuality and female independence unleashed by Selina Kyle.

The Catwoman is a recurrent figure in Hollywood cinema for the coding of female sexuality, notably in *Cat People* (1942) produced by Val Lewton. In comics by Miller and others, Selina Kyle is a lower-class hooker who first wears the cat costume for a client. In *Batman Returns* her PVC catsuit, designed appropriately by a New York sex shop and resembling a glass sculpture, contributes substantially to her grace and sensuality. Both Batman and Catwoman are fractured personalities, but the latter projects an image of female sexuality as powerful, enigmatic, and mythically linked with vampirism ('A kiss is deadly if you mean it') which can be interpreted as a desired but uncontrollable male fantasy of eroticism. Thus Batman is effectively dislodged in the irrational, polarised environment of the contemporary city.

The film's opening recalls American cinema's most notable tycoon, Charles Foster Kane, and in the power struggle which follows the principal villain is a ruthless corporate boss named Max Shreck, in homage to German actor Max Schreck who played the title role in Murnau's classic 1922 vampire film *Nosferatu*. Shreck feeds economically off the city and his proposed power plant will suck energy from it.

The expressionism evoked by Shreck/Schreck is extended to the subterranean Penguin lair with its echoes of the Phantom of the Opera, and to Gotham City which resembles Hugh Ferris's visions of a future Manhattan depicted in *The Metropolis of Tomorrow* (1929). His urban designs had considerable influence on Hollywood's interpretation of 'the city' in the 1930s. Ferris's skyscrapers are black megastructures as large and mysterious as Egyptian and Mayan pyramids. His city of monumental tombs inhabited by antlike people is contemporary with Lang's *Metropolis* in which sombre Expressionist architecture and the haunted spaces of medieval

Gothic produced a moribund city monitored by airships and planes. It anticipates Rivera's painting 'Frozen Assets: A Cross-Section Through the City ' (1931), in which the metropolis is seen as a mortuary where skyscrapers look like bombs. *Batman Returns*, therefore, draws on a substantial cinematic and cultural catalogue for its lurid images of urban chaos.

Shreck's hair and the padded leather interiors of his office are grey like the 'Machine Age Teutonic' statues which dominate Gotham Plaza. These monumental figures along with surrounding structures are patterned on totalitarian architecture, and more specifically upon Paul Manship's huge bronze of Prometheus at New York's Rockefeller Center of which the plaza is a pastiche. Ringed by Shreck's department store and looming government buildings, the Plaza is inhospitable and demoralising, with the Ice Rink and Xmas shopping humanising the scene and hinting at resistance through everyday practice. Rockefeller Plaza, a man-made, fabricated world is an appropriate model. While New York (Gotham City) symbolises urban America, so Rockefeller Center (Gotham Plaza) is a concentrated symbol of New York. Itself a sizeable city, populated daily by thousands of employees and visitors, it represents the zenith of the culture of congestion identified by Koolhaas. However, with its open public spaces, hedges and flower beds, and responsiveness to the fine arts (negative in the notorious case of the Diego Rivera mural, destroyed for its inclusion of Lenin), it has also in the past seemed to propose a kind of civic centre, more congenial than Gotham's equivalent. A more recent attempt to show the acceptable face of corporatism has conflated the iconic images of the caped crusader and the skyscraper. The South Central Bell building which dominates Nashville's skyline has outdoor plazas and a 'winter garden' atrium open to the public. Its most significant feature is its earpiece towers that themselves resemble miniature Moderne skyscrapers. Combined with an oval logo, these extrusions have fixed the local name of the edifice as 'the Batman building'.

One further inflection of the 'noir' film remains to be acknowledged. The study of genre has moved from a concern with repetition to an emphasis on difference. Internal modifications of forms have been cited and Colin McArthur in *Underworld USA* (1972) suggested the category of the gangster/thriller to accommodate the development and fluidity of the form. More recently in *Genre* (1980) Steve Neale, while drawing attention to the relation and reciprocity between repetition and difference, argues the importance of discourse in genre specification. While the 'noir' thriller has remained viable in the 1990s, its mood and characters have attached themselves to road movies such as *Guncrazy* and *True Romance* in which the dysfunctions and pathologies of urban life have seeped into the lonely spaces between cities. Law and gender discourses are supplemented by those of youth and rebellion. The landscape of motels, billboards, filling stations and desert wilderness may be different but the environment is still the repository of hatred and impending disaster. 'Like noir ... road movies are cowled in lurking menace, spontaneous mayhem and dead-end fatalism.'[15] The automobile becomes the 'metal coffin' of *Taxi Driver* when the highway becomes the jungle and a joyride a nightmare.

NOTES

1   D. Mazzoleni, 'The City and the Imaginary', *New Formations* 11 (Subjects in Space, Summer 1990), 100.

2   P. Schrader, 'Notes on Film Noir', *Film Comment*, 8:1, (Spring 1972), 11.

3   D. Reid and J. L. Walker, 'Strange Pursuit: Cornell Woolrich and the Abandoned City of the Forties' in J. Copjec (ed.), *Shades of Noir* (London/New York, Verso, 1993), pp. 74, 79.

4   *Ibid.*, p. 68.

5   C. Clarens, *Crime Movies: from Griffith to the Godfather and Beyond* (London, Secker and Warburg, 1980), p. 313.

6   I. Penman, 'Juke Box and Johnny Boy', *Sight and Sound* 3:4, (April 1993), 10, 11.

7   L. Quart and A. Auster, *American Film and Society since 1945* (New York, Praeger, 1991, Second Edition), p. 126.

8   P. Kael, *When the Lights Go Down* (London, Boyars, 1980), pp. 132–3.

9   L. Gross, 'Film Aprés Noir', *Film Comment*, 12:4 (July/August 1976), 45.

10   P. Wollen, 'Delirious Projections', *Sight and Sound*, 2:4, (August 1992), 25.

11   D. Harvey, *The Condition of Postmodernity* (Oxford, Blackwell, 1989), pp. 310, 311.

12   M. Davis, '*Chinatown*, Revisited?: The Internationalization of Downtown Los Angeles' in D. Reid (ed.), *Sex, Death and God in L.A.* (New York, Pantheon, 1992), p. 21.

13   W. Uricchio and R. E. Pearson, 'I'm Not Fooled By That Cheap Disguise', in Uricchio and Pearson (eds.), *The Many Lives of The Batman* (New York and London, Routledge/BFI, 1991), p. 206.

14   Wollen, 'Delirious Projections', 26.

15   M. Atkinson, 'Crossing the Frontiers', *Sight and Sound*, 4:1, (January 1994), 16.

7

CHICAGO

The mythic masculine image of the city of Chicago comprises work and crime: stockyards, packing houses and steel mills, now closed; guns and feuding gangsters also part of history. In the European consciousness shaped by Hollywood the Midwest city, dynamic and modern yet also decadent, was more familiar than New York. The gangster movie *Underworld* (1927) was released in France as *Les Nuits de Chicago*.

To residents and scholars it is a family town. Its immigrant neighbourhoods, with their wooden bungalows and cottages housing individual families, their shopping strips with announcements variously in Polish, Italian, Hebrew, Arabic, or Korean, and their Roman Catholic churches (many now marked for demolition) are among the most segregated in the United States, setting a pattern of behaviour that has buttressed widespread prejudice against Afro-Americans throughout the twentieth century. Within neighbourhoods closeness, an almost tribal solidarity, poses an obstacle to the unravelling of mysteries and the solution of crimes. Street names and food – King Drive, Emerald Avenue, Pulaski Road, soul food, Irish meat pies, kielbasa – testify to the influence of a succession of working-class ethnic inhabitants.

In those areas where the authority of the political machine governed individual behaviour, city employees eagerly joined civic bosses and court officials in graft and corrupt practices, supporting the charge implied in Nelson Algren's description of Chicago as the 'City on the Make.' Chicago's masculinism has also surfaced in the form of vigorous xenophobia, racism, and 'Red Scares' notably after World War I; the Chicago police riot of 1968 can be seen as a variant of such pathological manifestations. Sara Paretsky's Chicago crime novels, written from a liberal, feminist – and unsentimental – perspective, sometimes record the bigotry, racial, cultural and sexual, of the urban proletariat among other social groupings.[1]

Neighbourhoods had their own funeral parlours, pool halls, clubs, eccentrics, and taverns. The city's thousands of bars, like the Kilarney Tavern in Robert Campbell's *Boneyards* (1992) with its smells of corned beef, cabbage and beer-soaked wood, offering a version of European pub life. A main street every half mile enclosed residential streets. The existence of taverns and small grocery stores in side streets made long journeys unnecessary. Consequently families, especially during long winters, became urban villagers remaining within the ethnic enclave which was bounded by railway tracks, industries, rivers and thoroughfares.

In contrast to the flamboyance of the Irish in Bridgeport, the Poles, Croats and Slovaks injected a sullen, resigned element into the city's character, with the grim, melancholy lives of immigrant toilers being recorded at the turn of the century (1900) by Dreiser in *Sister Carrie*. Paretsky, the city's most celebrated crime novelist, uses her detective V. I. Warshawski to depict the inbred, parochial lives of these immigrants on South Chicago's East Side 'stuck in formaldehyde' since the presidency of Woodrow Wilson: 'Its members live in stubborn isolation, trying to recreate the Eastern European villages of their grandparents.'[2]

In fiction therefore Old Chicago's ugliness and rawness, as well as its family values and ancient foodways, lie behind the modern image of a dynamic, neon-lit metropolis planted in the midst of a limitless prairie. Les Roberts, most of whose novels are situated in a similar Midwest lakeside city, Cleveland, describes a parallel neighbourhood in *Pepper Pike* (1988) (the name of a new affluent suburb on the city's eastern edge). In Chapter 11 Roberts's Slovenian PI, Milan Jacovich journeys to a part of Greater Cleveland radically different from Pepper Pike to visit his aunt Branka who 'now lived in the three-bedroom lathe and wood house alone, cooking gigantic meals each night for her children, nieces and nephews, cousins, and the unacknowledged sisterhood of black-clad Slovenian widows'.[3] Branka is characteristic of a generation of older single women (many of them widows) who avoid the streets at night and who have no map of the city in their heads. There are exceptions, such as Warshawski's Aunt Elena in *Burn Marks* (1990), who, despite their erratic access to urban facilities, survive by means of cunning, luck and the generosity of others.

Founded on an unsuitable site, Chicago the 'silver city' of the nineteenth century was an artifice, a monument to will power. New York's Grid System (1807) which had sought to impose order on and subjugate the chaos of nature offered a model of resolution; to counter the flatness of the Midwest terrain and to announce that this wild environment could be tamed, soaring buildings were erected making Chicago a world capital of modern architectural landmarks. The Chicago School of Sullivan, Root, Burnham, Richardson and Frank Lloyd Wright simply created in the 1890s the principles of twentieth century public construction, inventing the 'curtain-wall', fire proofing and the Chicago window, and making the city a forest of skyscrapers before they were established in New York.

Chicago's reputation became that of a brawling, muscular town, one whose economic success was based in part on hustlers and magnates, and on steam machines which transported grain and handled pigs and cattle. The architects however were cosmopolitan, scholarly types who preferred ornate decoration to bare functionalism, an attitude which would lead to the embellishment of auditoriums and department stores with symbolism. The Public Library (1897) for instance has a glowing interior of mosaics and Tiffany skylights, while in Burnham and Root's Rookery Building (1886), also distinguished by its skylight (in iron and glass), the decoration emphasises the structure. This ornamentalism (especially in the form of terracotta) extended to domestic housing by the 1930s. In *Toxic Shock* (1988) V.I . Warshawski, exploring Nancy Cleghorn's home on Crandon near 73rd Street, notices the stained glass windows and cupolas on the corners.

The architectural splendour produced by Sullivan and Frank Lloyd Wright, both of whom delighted in geometric and vegetable design, was evoked in De Palma's vivid recreation of the Al Capone years, *The Untouchables* (1987), in which the mobster's banquet table and sumptuous hotel apartments fill the Panavision screen. Capone represents ethnicity betrayed and disgraced, as the rookie Italian–American cop (once Guiseppe Petri, now George Stone) ardently insists. The movie's grandiose style is supported by David Mamet's screenplay which takes Capone to the Chicago *Opera* House, Ness the FBI agent, and Malone, to a vast Catholic church, and concludes in the cavernous Union Station with its ornamental detail and rich marble staircase. This public and private opulence is brought into question by veteran cop Jim Malone's modest dwelling on

Racine with its well stocked bookcase and dime-store wallpaper. Yet as references to the end of Prohibition and to a new era in the city's history mark the end of the narrative, the final frames of massive urban architecture propose a guarantee of civic continuity.

Chicago is an inland city though it borders that huge expanse of water Lake Michigan, more a sea than a lake and a geographical feature with aesthetic and softening effects. The line of the lake shore exposing the metropolis to view is basic to any mapping of the city as indigenous Chicagoans would testify. In response to its high water table, Chicago built its first skyscrapers on floating rafts and jacked up other buildings over the surface sewer pipes, now a rat-infested refuge for the homeless in Paretsky's *Tunnel Vision*. Further-more the blue clay made the land marshy, a feature Paretsky draws on in *Guardian Angel* (1992) where the shadows of the old machines she encounters in the Diamond Head plant look like 'monsters from the primordial swamp that spawned Chicago' and in *Blood Shot* (*Toxic Shock* in the UK).

One of the key locations in the latter text is the grimly named Dead Stick Pond, part of an overflow of the Calumet River, once among the last wetlands in Illinois for migrant birds. The pond 'wasn't very deep, but its murky waters covered a vast expanse of the marsh.' Official signs deliver conflicting messages: the pond is both a federal clean water project (where herons and beavers con-tinue to live), and a repository for hazardous waste of various kinds. As the messages intersect, the project of ecological conservation, the practice of ethics, indicts the spread of pollution, the practice of criminality. Later Vic Warshawski, struggling to survive after being beaten and dumped in the pond, is assailed by the smell of chemicals mixed with the 'rank stench of putrefying grasses'.[4]

The pond is linked both geographically and thematically with the worn-out, rusting factories of South Chicago such as USX and Wisconsin Steel. This thoroughly depressed part of Chicago is haunted by memories of sailors, social reformers and the stock-yards. 'On the South Side is the detritus of de-industrialization: truck drivers whose terminals have closed, steelworkers living on government cheese, old men sipping Cokes in the bars at noon, young men drifting back from Houston to enrol in community colleges, disciples of Saul Alinsky picketing chemical dumps.'[5] One of those dumps is the Xerxes Chemical Plant at 110th Street east of Torrence, built like its neighbours on toxic clay dredged from Lake Calumet. Now a lunar landscape of oily mud surrounds the plant

whose interior provides one more evocation of Expressionist cinema. Xerxes is the malign centre which Warshawski must expose in
Toxic Shock and at the novel's climax she takes a dinghy on the
Calumet River to enter the plant unobserved. Fog on the river, the
acrid air, the absence of other humans apart from her temporary
companion Ms Chigwell, the industrial maze that is Xerxes – these
particulars create not only conventional narrative suspense but also
an aura of the dreamlike and Gothic.

Vic Warshawski 's roots are in the traditional blue-collar districts on Chicago's southern edge just north of Calumet City. As a
private investigator she is situated by successive narratives in the
downtown area: she rents a large, untidy apartment on Halsted
north of Belmont (it is revealed in *Deadlock*, 1984) not far from her
office in one of the South Loop buildings. Her investigations, using
the lake and Sears Tower as landmarks or the El tracks for orienta-
tion, contrive to be a topographical diagram of Chicago and its suburbs and often require automobile journeys on those expressways
(Kennedy, Eisenhower) radiating from the downtown core. On the
other hand, through Warshawski's explorations of desolate streets
and delapidated buildings, the text depicts landscapes familiar to the
poor who travel on foot or by bus. The descriptions of urban decay
in *Burn Marks* contribute to the portrayal of such landscapes.
Cermak Road (between Indiana and Halsted) once housed Chicago's
robber barons, the Fields, Sears and Armours. 'Today it consists of
vacant lots, auto dealers, public housing, and the occasional SRO
(Senior Residential Occupancy).' The dereliction is emphasised by
the pathetic attempt to restore some of the original mansions, the
'empty opulent shells' forming a 'macabre ghost town'.[6]

Compared with novels by Chandler or Hammett, the Paretsky
books project a more democratic public space in which the nature
and limits of female practices are articulated. Both generally as an
independent professional woman and in her literal role of detective,
Vic Warshawski propels a series of texts (the voice is first person)
that portray the experience of being female in the city. Although
she scorns the gentrification spreading from Lincoln Park, the
phenomenon is the consequence of male and female singles (as well
as gays and professional couples) being attracted to central urban
locations. The urban setting poses particular problems for single
women, chiefly those created by male authoritarianism; on the
other hand the city can offer economy and friendship. The social
network of women's spaces found in the contemporary city – coffee

shops, bookstores, bars – is more evident in lesbian crime novels such as Murder at the Nightwood Bar (1987) (Katherine V. Forrest) or Everything You Have is Mine (1992) (Sandra Scoppettone), but Guardian Angel in particular shows the sisterly solidarity that is available. At the Diamond Head machine assembly shop it is the female Spanish workers who offer information to Vic and protect her when the foreman questions her. Later, when she is pursued by murderous hoodlums, the waitresses at the Belmont Diner facilitate her escape, halting her pursuers by means of iced tea and a can of hot grease.

Although Paretsky's Burn Marks was published by Virago Press in the UK, she remains a fundamentally mainstream writer whose representations of female life are, consequently, restricted in certain ways. Though armed like Philip Marlowe with a Smith and Wesson, Warshawski never kills an enemy. Although Chicago's urban rape statistics are the highest in the nation she is never violated. Her fear is often represented by nausea or throwing up, but otherwise functions of the body (urinating at a stakeout, for instance) are ignored. In contrast, a call of nature and intense hunger interrupt Officer Langdon's surveillance of LaBelle Doucette's flat in Julie Smith's New Orleans Mourning (1990) 'she was damned if she was going to drop her jeans and pee in a corner of a burned-out house'.[7] More graphically Robert Campbell in Boneyards describes the effects on Wilda Sharkey's body of unstoppable terror, as she finds herself in the hours after midnight alone in the 'ravaged city' of Chicago, her condition exacerbated by the Hawk, the fierce freezing wind which scrapes her cheeks and chills her bladder:

> She could hear her urine splattering on the sidewalk, soiling her shoes.
> She could feel it wetting her legs and stockings.
> She could smell it, sharp with the smell of fear, as sharp as splintered bones in the nose.

The nature of the threat, economic and cultural, which Warshawski poses to the masculine world of criminals demands not her rape but her removal or elimination. Her opponents are unable to reconcile her profession and lifestyle with their simplistic categories of female sexuality. The aggressive manner in which she invades their male dominated organisations, such as a Catholic priory or corporate offices and plants, provokes their anger and resentment which spring from their own control obsessions and fantasies of violation by the 'other'. The insult of choice when a hoodlum is confronted by Warshawski is 'dyke'.

The dangers from women in early hard-boiled fiction by male authors are displaced by dangers to women. 'Women are never far from fear, night or day.' muses Wilda Sharkey, 'Never far from unexpected, unintended consequences following the most innocent excursions ...'[8] Looking for a witness – an indigent black woman Zerlina Ramsay – Warshawski is given an address: 'Sixteen hundred south Christiani is not in the happiest part of town. It's not a great place for any woman to be alone at night especially a white one.'[9] North Lawndale with its outcroppings of rubble, its broken or boarded windows, its abandoned cars in the purple twilight, is also a ghost town which features in Warshawski's bad dreams. Thus 'the intricacies of city life' provide Paretsky with 'a useful metaphor for the debilitating tensions of twentieth century life'.[10]

The core of the city is for Warshawski's work a crucial resource. It is there that individuals supply essential financial and legal information; it is there in the city that Warshawski, a divorcee and earlier an orphan, finds her surrogate family. Chicago remains the 'dazzling, alluring or disturbing spectacle' Dreiser described in *Sister Carrie*, enabling Warshawski to buy her Magli shoes, to relax in her favourite bar, The Golden Glow, and to admire the bronze wind chimes in front of the Standard Oil Building.

Like her male counterpart, the female private investigator is often an isolated figure prepared to answer violence with reciprocal violence. Warshawski's middle name is Iphigenia who in Greek legend was also Artemis the huntress. However her activities as investigator and solver of crimes fail to receive the accolade of patriarchal approval. Her communications with relatives and men (with whom she has to struggle to retain her sense of self) are problematised by their stereotyped view of gender roles. Warshawski's allegiance to the metropolis is by implication a criticism of lifestyles in the suburbs 'where the girls sit on a blanket waiting for the boys to finish talking business and to bring them drinks'.[11] As in the Victorian period the street (profane) is opposed to the home (sacred). For a woman to pursue a career in the public domain of the streets – and thus beyond the confines of the home – remains, from a 'respectable' and patriarchal standpoint, an affront to morality and decency, even an example of urban pathology. Discovered in the stairwell after midnight by a banker who lives in the same building, Vic is accused (in *Burn Marks*) of being a drug dealer and, like one of the women loitering in Benjamin's Parisian arcades, a prostitute.

Relevant to the feminism of Paretsky's novels is David Sibley's expansion of the picture of masculinist prejudice in *Geographies of Exclusion* (1995), where he argues that the radical social work and research among Chicago's poor, carried out by Jane Addams and her female colleagues at Hull House in the first decades of the twentieth century, were denigrated by several male sociologists at the University of Chicago, notably Robert Park. Recent correspondence between Dr Sibley and Peter Jackson, the humanistic geographer, reveals that the distinction between 'scientific' sociology (male) and social work (female), which encouraged Park to pronounce that Jane Addams and her kind were worse than criminals, still marginalises the latter profession. This separation and the attitudes responsible can be placed in an ironic context by the acknowledgement of the social work aspects of the career of the fictional detective, both female and male.

Chicago has a history of working-class radicalism and political disturbance. The antecedents of Sara Paretsky include socialist grandparents and great aunts who participated in the Russian revolution. As a student at the University of Chicago, her literary creation Vic Warshawski became a liberal: anti-war, feminist, pro-choice and anti-racist. Logically therefore, Paretsky agonised during the writing of *Burn Marks* about the negative characterisation of a black heroin addict, Cerise. Yet Warshawski understands the sullen, distrustful behaviour of a black woman confronted by a white stranger (Vic) conversant with the institutions of law and society which terrify her. Furthermore Terry Finchley, a black police officer, is one of the few men with whom Warshawski has a relationship of mutual understanding and respect, and in *Guardian Angel* she begins an affair with Conrad Rawlings, also a black cop.

Following the tradition of the petit bourgeois American PI Vic Warshawski rejects the affluence of the middle classes and of corporate business. Like Philip Marlowe she has an office in a down-market area, in her case on the southeast fringe of the Loop. 'Buildings around there don't fare too well. They're too close to the lockup, the slums, the peepshows and the cheap bars, so they attract clients like me: detectives on a shoestring budget, bail bondsmen, inept secretarial services.'[12] The El train rattles the windows of the Pulteney Building where the elevators are temperamental and the lavatories usually broken. Marlowe's dust-filled room and a half in West Hollywood contains five filing cabinets, a glass-topped desk and a nondescript rug. Vic's olive furnishings are from police auctions and secondhand shops, but although her Georgia O'Keeffe posters are an echo of Marlowe's Rembrandt calendar, her office is a more purely functional space than Marlowe's, which doubles as a second home in which to reflect on cases or to register from the seventh floor the disturbing scents of the sultry modern city.

In her pursuit of justice V.I. Warshawski is opposed to those described elsewhere (by myself) as 'corrupt politicians, decadent plutocrats, careless industrialists, brutal politicians and slimy hoodlums.'[13] Disillusioned by her work at the public defender's office, Vic's personal war on the rich and powerful who manipulate the legal system – from machine politicians to Mafia bosses – is directed at white collar criminals, not only financial crooks but also those who prey on the marginalised needy and elderly; fraudulent and incompetent doctors (*Bitter Medicine*); redevelopers turned arsonists (*Burn Marks*); businessmen rifling pension funds and junk bond salesmen (*Guardian Angel*).

In the opening of *Deep Shaker* (1992) Les Roberts describes a bitterly cold afternon at a football game in Cleveland's Municipal Stadium. The temperature is only 26 above zero. Like the Hawk the wind howls in from Lake Erie, and a stinging rain falls at a 45-degree angle. The effects of comparable weather conditions on the body and psyche in Chicago, 'the Windy City', have already been observed. Such conditions as they appear in the texts of *Deep Shaker* and Stuart Kaminsky's *Liebermann's Folly* (1991), set in Chicago, may only constitute local colour ; but in Paretsky's *Killing Orders* winter and the silent frozen lake provide symbols representing the selfishness and hostility of the novel's selfish and coldly ruthless characters.

The willpower and resilience which fostered the establishment and growth of Chicago animates Midwestern detectives such as Warshawski and Jacovich, as well as the maverick Irish cop, Ray Sharkey in *Boneyards*. Nicknamed the City Hall Pimp for his extra-curricular (and extra-legal) activities, Sharkey, with a wife who takes four years to die of cancer and a retarded daughter in an institution since childhood, is a man of troubles and sorrows. Targeted by 'The Candidate' who seeks to expose him as an example of police corruption and venal government, Sharkey turns the tables humiliating his enemies in the process.

In the book's final chapter, Sharkey, known around the area as a fashion plate, dresses in full uniform complete with 'ribbons of commendation and valor' to attend his trial for murder. The episode is captured in unusually naturalistic detail to emphasise the proud sense of self felt by Campbell's protagonist, a man whose clothes are cut to remind him of 'body attitude, strength and posture'. It is the physical challenge of Chicago and its climate which is evoked in Sharkey's boldest moment. To temporarily hide a bribe at a party, he plunges the blue envelope containing the notes into a tub half-filled with chilled cans of beer – under the floating ice, a synecdoche for the city in winter.

NOTES

1   Cf. *Guardian Angel* (London, Penguin, 1992), p. 370: ' The conversation [in Barney's working class bar] turned to the usual complaints of the helpless, over the niggers and lesbians and Japs and everyone else who was ruining the country.'

2   S. Paretsky, *Toxic Shock* (London, Penguin, 1990), p. 34.

3   L. Roberts, *Pepper Pike* (London, Coronet, 1990), p. 117.

4   Paretsky, *Toxic Shock*, pp. 103, 174.

5   T. Geoghegan, 'Chicago, Pride of the Rustbelt', *The New Republic*, 25 March 1985, 20.

6   S. Paretsky, *Burn Marks* (New York, Dell, 1991), p. 14.

7   J. Smith, *New Orleans Mourning* (New York, Ivy Books, 1990), p. 181.

8   R. Campbell, *Boneyards* (New York, Pocket Books, 1993), pp. 204, 188.

9   Paretsky, *Burn Marks*, p. 164.

10   Jane S. Bakerman, 'Living "Openly and with dignity" — Sara Paretsky's New-Boiled Feminist Fiction, *MidAmerica* xii (Yearbook of the Society for the Study of Midwestern Literature), 1985, 12.

11   Paretsky, *Burn Marks*, p. 48.

12   S. Paretsky, *Killing Orders* in *Indemnity Only and Killing Orders* (London, Victor Gollancz, 1992), p. 29.

13   R. Willett, *Hard-Boiled Fiction* (Halifax, Ryburn/ British Association for American Studies,1992), p. 7.

8

NEW ORLEANS

As a recent and continuing Southern Comfort advertising campaign has demonstrated New Orleans is a seductive world to be captured in suggestive late night photos of jazz, hustling, dance, transgression and desire. To the rest of Louisiana, New Orleans is Sin City where guns rule the streets, money is respected more than death and sex, and Desire is one of the most dangerous housing 'projects' in the whole state.

Poverty and decay surround the romantic, classy Garden District which clings to its French and Spanish origins; Desire, also the name of a street, runs parallel with Piety in the Fourth Ward. Such contrasts are typical. Elegant and decadent, New Orleans is a site of contradictions, of luxury and decline, of beauty and brutality, of Christianity and paganism. Its affluent, uptown establishment, anatomised in the short stories of Ellen Gilchrist ('Rich', 'In the Land of Dreamy Dreams'), supports a gossipy, inbred social life that feeds on deviations from an underlying conservatism.

Discovered by the Spanish, founded by the French, ceded in turn to both nations, New Orleans was a Latin, European city for a century before it was sold to the USA. Its reputation among travellers in the nineteenth century was that of a Babylon where Creoles, Europeans and Americans gambled, danced and drank. Catholic holidays in the city have sought to combine spirituality and festivity, and its history of carnivals, parades and dances has generated the production of cultural images (New Orleans funerals, Mississippi steamboats, old-time jazzmen, the wrought iron façades of French Quarter houses) radically different and distanced from those prevailing in Protestant (and puritan) centres. Set in New Orleans and New England, Alan V. Hewat's award-winning novel

Lady's Time (1985) embodies that contrast in both structure and meaning.

Its inhabitants live comfortably with the mythology that dominates the national perception of the city and enjoy reconstructing the legends which permeate its literature, history, and food. 'Time ran over itself in layers in the liquid air of New Orleans, for there was no place to set the past aside; ... '¹ A wanderer in the city might pass from the nineteenth century of the so-called French Quarter, largely Spanish and Italian, to the eighteenth century of the Spanish Cabildo or state-house with its traces of the Middle Ages. Umberto Eco in *Travels in Hyperreality* developed this observation, arguing that since New Orleans is not in the neurosis of a denied past, it does not have to pursue 'the real thing'.

Beneath the trappings which attract tourism continuously, there exists a standard American metropolis with urban problems and bland suburbs. Like comparable cities in the North, New Orleans is disfigured by crime, drugs, traffic, race and unemployment. The port is decaying, the oil market depleted, the French Quarter run down, and the famous department store D. H. Holmes out of business. A vision of economic success by means of blackjack on riverboats and casinos along the lakefront has led to the introduction of legalised gambling: in Dick Lochte's *Bayou Blue* (1992) a dead PI's cryptic scribble 'New At C' is decoded as 'New Atlantic City'.

Describing the eastern district of Gentilly, Walker Percy's protagonist Binx Bolling in *The Moviegoer* (1961) announces, 'Except for the banana plants and the curlicues of iron in the Walgreen drugstore one would never guess it was part of New Orleans.'² Adrift and disconnected he is a seeker, existentially searching for meaning and identity. To observe the local scene and to watch others he becomes a kind of *flâneur*/detective and reports, 'I wander seriously [in the neighbourhood]'. New Orleans with its balconies and walled-off courtyards enables the observer to be stationed at a remove from the surrounding urban bustle. But Binx cannot continue to keep his distance. He is drawn into the maelstrom of the mass society whose lost souls he has perceived. Binx, who will marry, move to the Garden District and become a doctor, is part of that ordinary public in New Orleans and of its popular culture, using the movies to describe individuals and their dreams.

Certain characters in Chris Wiltz's crime novels, especially *The Emerald Lizard* (1991), affect Western clothes and speech. New Orleans though remains a city of the South, sharing in the region's sectional and racial history and myths. On one hand it is 'a land where the male leads are played by Clark Gable and Don Ameche, tipping their top hats , and escorting ladies to the ice-cream parlor.'³ On the other it is the exotic home of Mardi Gras , a festival which the Irish used to regard in the 1860s as 'get Nigger day'. Photographs of Robert E. Lee are dusted off for display in the windows of antique shops and Stars and Bars flags are everywhere. To the Afro-American writer Ishmael Reed, Mardi Gras is a decadent, Confederate pageant; one reason, he speculates, why the populist Governor of Louisiana, Huey Long, sought to eradicate it.

Long would never have been admitted to élite krewes (carnival organisations) such as Rex or Comus, whose Mardi Gras Kings and Queens are selected by the city's social élite which controls its economic and political life. The practice, during the parades, of 'royalty' throwing beads and trinkets to the public is an accurate reflection of class divisions when economic power is concentrated inside a small oligarchy. 'The private world of social hierarchy [is] symbolized by Mardi Gras. The élite, at least until recent years, has been an insular, traditionalist New Orleans born and bred group, in which family and inheritance have meant more than wealth.'⁴ For the St Amant family in Julie Smith's *New Orleans Mourning* (1990) Mardi Gras, when the city becomes a theatre without walls, facilitates an extension of their flamboyant, melodramatic and grotesque lifestyle. Rich, powerful, unhappy and desperate they are compared to the TV characters in *Dynasty*. The killing of Chauncey St Amant, King of Carnival, as the Rex Parade moves down St Charles Avenue, invites an investigation of the family which uncovers a history of hatreds, prejudices, drunkenness, violence, promiscuity, transvestism and racism.

After her rebellion against the privileged upbringing she shares with the St Amants, Police Officer Skip Langdon becomes aware that she is neither part of police culture nor a member of 'the old crowd'. Her mediating position however enables a contrast to be made between the aristocratic milieu and the 'real' world of New Orleans. She had longed to go to neighbourhoods she hardly knew and 'truly meet the people'. Subsequently, when she travels to the Garden District to conduct interviews after the murder, her habitual dread of the area elicits a comparison with the ghetto of Tremé from where the black call girl LaBelle Doucette, sent away as a baby into exile and poverty, emerges and invades the Garden District bent on blackmail. Her intended target Chauncey summarily strangles her. Individual members of the family act without restraint according to desire or social position and a web of complicity conceals acts of cruelty and immorality. The Gaynauds, their counterparts in *Blue Bayou*, are another grand, upper-class family, less extreme but, hiding in St Charles behind their green shutters and false flambeaux, their gnarled oaks and filigree iron fence, similarly at pains to conceal a sordid past of miscegenation and violence.

From the perpective of Bakhtin and his followers, Carnival holds the potential for protest and resistance. Traditionally Mardi Gras has accommodated satire and mockery, notably in the activities of Black Indians and drag queens. Other scholars have maintained that the ritualizing of possible disruption is the essential and cathartic function of Carnival, so the licensing of transgression appears to be a strategy enabling power to consolidate itself. The shooting of the King by 'Dolly Parton' in *New Orleans Mourning* suggests parody, but the novel as a whole does not offer a straightforward illustration or endorsement of either interpretation. However, although the narrative demonstrates the disintegration of the St Amants, a conspiracy of social power (the mayor, the DA and the Police Chief) destroys the evidence which could demonstrate that Chauncey was killed by his alcoholic wife.

The book's major ironies are connected with New Orleans cultural history and with race. LaBelle is not, as the text at first suggests, the offspring of a white master–black slave relationship and therefore the modern equivalent of the literary 'tragic octoroon'. Chauncey has extra-marital affairs but he himself is the octoroon figure and Bitty, Chauncey's wife, is the mother of LaBelle, originally Hélène. The second irony is that Chauncey, who represents the élite crew, Rex, at Mardi Gras, is elected by the Boston Club which excludes Jews, Afro-Americans and 'ethnics'. The Zulu Parade of Afro-Americans sprang up as a response to Rex, its first members being porters and labourers. Despite his support for Civil Rights and for music in the city (including black jazz) Chauncey denies his racial origins in a vain attempt to cling on to dominance, the prerogative of the white power structure. In different circumstances Chauncey would be the black servant leading the parade horses for Rex or Comus, in contrast to the Black Indians who, by adopting an Afro-Caribbean performance style, challenge in a spirit of black pride the stereotypes of Africans and, significantly, Amerindians. 'The adaptation by blacks of the Indian persona was an act of ritual rebellion ... It was the highest compliment the African could pay a race of the New World; it stemmed from common struggle, sociocultural intercourse, a shared vision of freedom.'[5]

The various activities which make up the carnival and last for more than a month establish the city's uniqueness while under-lining other features of the city, such as its close-knit exclusiveness. The élite krewes keep their methods of arriving at guest lists secret while the chants of the Mardi Gras Indians are often based on a secret coded language. Street directions, given as lake, river, uptown, downtown, imply a shared knowledge. Southernness also supplies provinciality with whole families, especially in the Irish Channel, living in the same block for generations like Midwestern immi-grants.

The physical and psychological geography of the city is virtu-ally that of an island, a separate place, hidden within the crescent of the treacherous, polluted Mississippi and surrounded by swamp-land. Neal Rafferty, the PI in *The Emerald Lizard* by Chris Wiltz, puts this in perspective as he drives south of the river towards Lafitte and Barataria, and sees the endangered wetlands, eroded by storms and oil company dredging: 'There are times when New Or-leans can seem like the end of the earth because it is so isolated, so different from other cities ... but New Orleans is the center of the universe compared to the feeling I got from the marsh.' On a hot day that feeling, 'a weird kind of open-air entrapment',[6] is compar-able to the oppressiveness felt by characters in New Orleans crime novels. Jean Lafitte used the waterways to hide and escape after acts of smuggling and piracy so, as that romantic history suggests, they constitute a landscape as labyrinthine and therefore mystifying as any urban scene.

Within the borders of the urban island there are internal psychological barriers, such as Magazine Street (in *The Killing Circle*) and the bridge that joins the city to McDonoghville and the black projects (in *Blue Bayou*). The former separates and makes inverted mirror images of the genteel, shady Garden District and the tough, treeless Irish Channel, the breeding ground for the New Orleans Police Department. A more cynical view of the spatial rela-tionship is given by the black PI, Lew Griffin in *The Long-Legged Fly* (1992): 'Whenever it rained, which in New Orleans was damn near always, water poured down from the Garden District just uptown onto the poor, low-living Irish here [in the Channel] ... '[7]

Skip Langdon's principal distinction is between the Vieux Carré and the Garden District. While Dave Robichaux in *The Neon*

Rain (1987) describes the latter conventionally in terms of its scrolled and pillared homes, bordered by clipped lawns, and its blaze of flowers, shrubs and trees, Skip, temporarily charmed by old-fashioned gaslights and the smell of magnolia and jasmine, still considers it as evil and dangerous as Tremé. Repelled by the ubiquitous interior decor, 'wing-chair-and-Audubon-print', and stifled by the thick and smothering atmosphere outside, she renames it Rappaccini's District after Hawthorne's sinister scientist. And it is there in the District that Robichaux tracks down retired General Abshire now engaged in funding right-wing adventures in Central America. In contrast she loves the variety of the French Quarter which encompasses tawdriness, delapidated elegance and a street life guaranteed by its poor but resilient inhabitants.

Rafferty and Robichaux (in *The Neon Rain*) inevitably perceive the Quarter from a police perspective; most of the time it is for them a lunatic asylum, its residents transvestites, junkies, winos and prostitutes. Unlike the *flâneur* enraptured by the visual spectacle of the public, they are seduced by the smells of the Vieux Carré. Rafferty finds that a cool morning in the Quarter when pastel colours shine in the sun yields a dampness that smells like fresh parsley. Watermelons, canteloupes, and strawberries in crates, and poor boy sandwiches 'dripping with shrimp and oysters',remind Robichaux of the small Creole town on Bayou Teche where he was born. And in *A Morning for Flamingos* (1990), on returning to the Quarter he gives a sensuous description of its small grocery stores, '... wood floors, ceiling fans, display coolers loaded with cheeses, sausages and skinned catfish, and bins of plums and bananas set out on the sidewalk under the colonnade'.[8] A survey of his new living environment similarly combines attractive physical details with – in place of enticing food – lush plants and vegetation.

For those people who inhabit the core of the city, the West Bank is as remote as a distant planet, with the exception of Algiers which still resembles New Orleans architecturally. The rest is regarded as a typical development of suburbs and commercial strips, and as Rafferty concedes, depressing trailer parks. On the other hand Rafferty, in search of The Emerald Lizard Lounge, gains a sense of adventure when his map tells him that 4th Street is part of the Old Spanish Trail. Investigating the incineration of the lounge and the death of its owner, he visits her house in Westwego, a Fifties suburb laid out in characteristic grid fashion. What distinguishes Westwego is that cars are secondary to the boats lodged under most of the carports: fishing boats, flat boats and several pirogues used for duck hunting. As the PI insists earlier in the text, 'In the end we're all from the same hot bayou country.'

Originally a ramshackle colony constructed below sea level, the city is as vulnerable as its Californian counterparts. The encroachment of the Gulf of Mexico assisted by hurricanes, heavy rainfall and subsequent floods has been a persistent fear sustaining the fantasy of urban destruction. In addition epidemics of cholera, typhus, yellow fever and malaria ravaged the metropolis in the mid-nineteenth century so that it became known as the graveyard of the nation.

The exuberance and violence of Mardi Gras is followed inevitably by the solemnity of Ash Wednesday: 'In New Orleans, where one takes a bus marked "Cemeteries" down Canal Street when going towards Metairie, and where one of the major streets is named "Elysian Fields"' the awareness of death gives rise to a local melancholy which merges with the city's air of faded romance.[9] Even exclusive suburban homes with their Australian pines and handsome coloured façades are represented in The Moviegoer as forlorn: 'A sadness settles over them like a fog from the lake'. A similar perception in Julie Smith's New Orleans Mourning underlines the European connection; on the day of Chauncey St Amant's funeral, the vision of a sunlit girl, with an air of being forgotten, on the porch of a run-down 'double shotgun' house constitutes for his daughter Marcelle a moody artistic scene. The building is 'badly in need of a paint job' in more ways than one, preferably by an Impressionist such as Degas who lived for a time in New Orleans.

While funerals, ghosts, and superstition nourish New Orleans's mystical image, the community is fortified by particular rituals such as the jazz funeral and All Saints Day (November 1) when citizens visit, decorate and clean the graves of families and friends. At the focal point of such ceremonies are the centrally located cemeteries, themselves resembling cities of the dead and making the metropolis one vast floating necropolis. The cemetery is for Foucault another heterotopia, one which, increasingly associated with illness, becomes moved to the borders of cities. In New Orleans though its cemeteries remain the sacred heart of the city. They include Metairie where Chaucey St Amant is buried, the family estate of monuments symbolising old Creole New Orleans just as the St Amants embody the collective and historical guilt of the South.

A murder and subsequent funeral are the occasion, in The Emerald Lizard, for a description of the best known cemetery, St.

Louis Number One near the French Quarter: 'It's the oldest cemetery in the city, hundreds of crumbling, whitewashed tombs like tiny buildings, standing above the ground, safe houses for the dead so they're kept high and dry in a city that barely keeps itself above sea level.'[10] As Wiltz reports, the cemetery, now one of the most dangerous areas in the city, contains what is supposedly the tomb of Marie Laveau, the 'voodoo queen'. Bones, hair and dolls are left there, even a body accompanied by some form of gris-gris.

In *The Long-Legged Fly*, the first signs of day in New Orleans are compared to the horror film scene in which the hand of a corpse opens and closes. The city's mythology of Carnival, piracy and voodoo has been embraced by popular culture notably when the crime text has inclined towards the genre of Gothic.

Latin society allowed slaves to keep more of their old culture: vodun which celebrated African gods was kept alive by private ceremonies and by musical entertainments on Sundays in Congo Square. Just as the blood lines of black and white, African and European would merge so Afro-Americans and others mixed vodun and Catholicism. Vodun distinguished New Orleans from other areas of slavery as effectively as Mardi Gras with which it shares a number of characteristics: dancing and drumming, ritual masking and costuming, and polytheistic rites. Performed in whorehouses, jazz was generated by vodun which, as Hoodoo became, in the perspective of poet and novelist Ishmael Reed, an alternative American multiculturalism; well-known madams included Mammy Pleasant and Marie Laveau who, like Dr John, was known for good works. In vodun, a religion without a devil, the houngan or priest was admired for his healing qualities .

Popular culture, in such films as *The Big Easy* (1986) and *Angel Heart* (1987), only succeeded in vulgarising the religion as black magic, an occult form of devil worship involving, in the latter, chickens' feet and ripping out the heart of a victim. This is vodun (or more usually 'voodoo') for tourists, augmented in *Angel Heart* – New Orleans replaces the New York of William Hjortsberg's 1978 novel – by dark, expressionist shadows, tap-dancing on wet pavements, and decaying Southern mansions. *Angel Heart* is more significant for its self-conscious presentation of the hard-boiled formula which moves it, in the manner of Jim Thompson and Cornell Woolrich, towards supernatural horror, as the names of the detective, Harry Angel, and of his nemesis, Louis Cyphre (Lucifer), indicate.

The conventional metropolitan environment becomes satanic. The hard-boiled plot, apparently labyrinthine, is revealed as circular, the detective creating mystery since he is his own prey. Hunter and hunted murderer are identical. The map that leads to a solution is Angel's own history. The city is only a backcloth though ironically the fatalistic text of this ghoulish exercise in *film noir* becomes another expression of New Orleans's melancholic association with death.

The wall of cypress and vine extends to Lake Pontchartrain, a reminder that the primitive wilderness of Louisiana lies outside, shrouding the flat city and inducing claustrophobia but also invading its consciousness. The Garden District, described as an elegant corpse, is transformed into a dark segment of the forest, evoking the plantations beyond with their gloomy oaks and the swamps with their mists, fetid odours and eerie sounds. Thus both the city and its hinterland generate a sense of the Gothic across a variety of literary forms including vampire narratives (Anne Rice) and crime fiction.

Characteristic of the Garden District in particular are dream-like, decaying mansions. The private investigator Neal Rafferty (in *The Emerald Lizard*) finds a second floor apartment in 'a giant old cypress house' uptown with 'fourteen-foot ceilings, mantel pieces and the smell of musk that becomes part of all those old New Orleans dwellings'.[11] The low, rusted fence and the flaking paint contribute to the haunting sense of dereliction. Rafferty's recognition of the atmosphere conditions his response to the environment which, with its traces of the past, he finds satisfyingly comfortable. On a visit to Audubon Park, Dave Robichaux is similarly assuaged by a glistening green streetcar and the misty trees on St Charles; 'the smoky neon signs, the bright rain-streaked windows of the restaurant and the drugstore on the corner were like part of a nocturnal painting out of the 1940s'.[12] The protagonist's reverie, creating an artificial, romantic image of the modern city complete with American icon (the corner drugstore) constitutes a dangerous misreading. Robichaux's slackness renders him vulnerable and, although the above description contains sufficient warning references to *film noir*, he is easily ambushed at his girl-friend's door by several murderous gun-smugglers. Among the more popular myths of the city recently are those of New Orleans as a woman, either as Southern belle or courtesan (or both); in *The Neon Rain* it temporarily assumes the form and role of a Hollywood *femme fatale* .

Lew Griffin in James Sallis's *The Long-Legged Fly* is more

familiar with the New Orleans of the Quarter and, across the river, those parts of Algiers where driveways are filled with junked cars, oil drums and abandoned refrigerators. Sallis's writing brings together the tradition of the male Afro-American novel perpetuated in the crime fiction of Himes and Mosley with the weary, cynical post-Vietnam strain of hard-boiled fiction (Estelman, Crumley, Valin, Burke). *The Long-Legged Fly* lays out the social condition and psychology of an urban PI in a context of race, with Sallis sharing some of Mosley's insights into masculinity while transferring the action to New Orleans.

For Griffin as for Rawlins the priority is survival, the black self jeopardised not just by professional dangers but by problems involving character, sexuality and identity. Both men are tormented by their own demons, by anger and an urge to violence they know they must suppress. Rawlins's relations with women are marked by aggression, even sadism; Griffin is self-effacing, nervous of commitment so that finally in 1990 (the narrative's various periods, beginning in 1964, are precise) his long term friend Verne accuses him of treating women as interchangeable. He is at least attentive to the black culture of George Schuyler, Chester Himes and Bessie Smith which articulates his condition. The blues, as explained by a TV programme he watches on PBS, is interpreted as a means of getting beyond and therefore dealing with pain, disillusion, rage and loss, but Griffin acknowledges that when he feels the urge to kill pimps and pornographers, the hellhounds of bluesman Robert Johnson are snapping at his heels.

His agenda is to prevent individuals including himself sinking into the abyss of drink, drugs, self-loathing and despair that terminates in death or madness. In the melancholy urban world created by Sallis, black people simply disappear, to be found, if at all, dying in a ghetto apartment or raving in a state hospital, like Corene Davis, Sixties black activist, whose spiralling decline begins when she assumes the identity of a white hooker.

Griffin is saved by love and charity, and by attaining a different identity. New Orleans, he discovers is 'a constructed city, dredged out of swampland by sheer force of will and labor, nibbled at constantly by history, the river, the swamp's dark mouth'.[13] Arbitrarily, almost casually, he takes up a new and successful career as a crime novelist, inventing a Cajun detective Boudleaux (a reference presumably to Robichaux) who operates in the 'constructed city'. The once improvised narratives start to incorporate increasingly the (invented) experiences and history of Griffin himself – as though these fictions could, by drawing upon the life of the fictional writer, achieve a different level of authenticity. This postmodern playfulness which salutes another minority group is displaced by commodification in the end papers of the Avon paperback edition. Facing the end of the narrative is a full page advertisement headed: Cajun Crime/ Featuring Dave Robichaux/By Edgar Award Winning Author/ James Lee Burke.

With the assimilation of Cajun materials crime fiction capital-ises upon a continuing interest in minority ethnic groups while maintaining, especially in urban texts, the tradition of lonely, alien-ated modern man. The procedure also signals a romantic nostalgia encouraged by New Orleans. Burke's Cajun, Robichaux, is susceptible to that nostalgia, but stays clear-sighted about the moral squalor of Cajun behaviour, 'organized dogfights and cockfights, the casual attitude towards the sexual exploitation of Negro women, the environmental ignorance that allowed the draining and industrial pollution of the wetlands'.[14] On the other hand Lochte's Cajuns out at Blue Bayou are a vanishing race, an elegiac image of a rural past and a separate, fragile culture of music, language, folkways and food. The change of name from Ciel Bleu Bayou to Blue Bayou is part of the cultural process that includes the commodification of Cajun cuisine.

Cajun culture performs different roles for characters in the city. The opera-loving hitman Foster Fouchette loathes zyedeco but uses the final line of a Cajun song for fake suicide notes: 'I got nothing more to lose'. At the wake following Fouchette's funeral, the detective and protagonist Terry Manion asks the band to play that song 'Final Lament' which exorcises the painful memory of his best friend (and mentor) J.J. Legendre, assassinated in the prologue by Fouchette – ironically 'a fellow Frenchman'. In the New Orleans crime novel, popular music in the form of bland, diluted Dixieland is often used to register the city's commercialisation and decline. The ending of *Blue Bayou* presents to Manion's consciousness the other half of the equation: laughter, food and drink; tall tales of the mystical bayou; and at the end of the evening a forlorn ballad that paradoxically bestows health and exhilaration.

NOTES

1   A.V. Hewat, *Lady's Time* (New York, Ballantine Books, 1985), p. 69.
2   W. Percy, *The Moviegoer* (New York, Popular Library, 1961), p. 11.
3   I. Reed, *Shrovetide in Old New Orleans* (Garden City, N. Y., Doubleday,1978), p. 25.
4   V. H. Bryan, 'Land of Dreams: Image and Reality in New Orleans', *Urban Resources* 1 (Spring, 1984), 32.
5   J. Berry, J. Foose, T. Jones, *Up From the Cradle of Jazz: New Orleans Music Since World War II* (Athens, Ga; U. of Georgia Press, 1986), p. 210.
6   C. Wiltz, *The Emerald Lizard* (New York, Dutton/NAL,1991), p. 143.
7   J. Sallis, *The Long-Legged Fly* (New York, Avon Books, 1992), p. 13.
8   J. L. Burke, *A Morning For Flamingos* (New York, Avon Books,1991), p. 59.
9   Bryan, 'Land of Dreams', 31.
10 Wiltz, *Emerald Lizard*, pp. 98-9.
11 *Ibid.*, p. 243.
12 J. L. Burke, *The Neon Rain* (London, Mysterious Press, 1989), p. 37.
13 Sallis, *Long-Legged Fly*, p. 86.
14 Burke, *Morning For Flamingos*, p. 227.

CRIME, POPULAR CULTURE AND URBAN DESTINY

> Cities, like dreams, are made of desires and fears, even if the
> thread of their discourse is secret, their rules are absurd, their
> perspectives deceitful, and everything conceals something
> else. (Italo Calvino, *Invisible Cities*)

The preceding chapters have not exhausted those urban locations
which feature in American crime fiction. Robert B. Parker's hard-
boiled narratives take place in Boston with the author drawing on
historically resonant New England place-names, to contrast the lost
agrarian America and innocent young Republic of the Founding Fathers with the garish, violent United States of the 1980s. Upon returning from a trip to Washington DC the seat of government and
its scheming politicians, Parker's hero Spenser looks up...

> to the top of State Street where the old South Meeting House
> stood, soft red birch with, on the 2nd floor, the icon of unicorn
> carved and gleaming in gold leaf adorning the building as they
> had when the Declaration of Independence was read from its
> balcony and before it, the street where Crispus Attucks had
> been shot. It was a little like cleansing the palate.[1]

The sentimental nostalgia to which hard-boiled texts are vulnerable is here, in *The Widening Gyre*, given a nationalistic and (in the
reference to Crispus Attucks, black martyr in the Boston Massacre
of 1770) impeccably 'liberal' flavour. In *She Came Too Late* (1986)
Mary Wings, through her central character Emma Victor, challenges
the apparent stability of Parker's Boston. In this text the reactionary
city is 'a sinking ship, women and children going down first'. As a
lesbian and as a worker at the Women's Hotline, Emma transgresses
the boundaries of sexuality, class, geography and information to

reveal the economic and social constraints imposed by a city where a hostile patriarchy governs.

As in Sara Paretsky's novels, the primary boundary for women is that between the domestic, bourgeois world and the workplace, in this instance the Hotline and the Blackstone Clinic for Women. A major patriarchal site, and home to the rich and famous, Stanley Glassman's mansion, where stained glass panels decorate the freshly painted back door, is breached by Emma during her investigations, thus recalling similar populist intrusions by Chandler's Marlowe. The narrative explores, among other topics, sexual politics, fertility and squeezing the unions. Its various portrayals emphasise the centrality of work and power to the experience of women in the city, where crucial knowledge can be gained from female support and interaction, for which the Hotline is an important metaphor.

Knowledge for survival is passed on in Lisa Cody's *Monkey Wrench* (1994) when wrestler Eva Wylie agrees to give a group of London prostitutes lessons in self-defence. Eva's American counterpart in Peter Blauner's *Casino Moon* (1994) is Rosemary Giordano who triumphs over the fascism of the male audience ('their voices like storm troopers' boots on the tarmac') by sexually humiliating their drunken, lecherous representative in the ring. The casinos are those of Atlantic City which, like the better known gambling town of Las Vegas, provides particular opportunities for crime fiction. Louis Malle's film *Atlantic City, USA* (1981) achieves an hallucinatory style which accommodates both ironic nostalgia and hopeful fairytales. At the casino a girl group sings, 'On the Boardwalk at Atlantic City / Life will be peaches and cream.' Later, a hospital official, opening the Frank Sinatra wing of the local Medical Center begins his speech with the words: 'I have a vision of the future. This glorious island of Atlantic City, shining like a beacon ...' Not all fairytales come true. As he speaks Sally, the would-be croupier whom Lou seeks to 'protect', walks through the suite on her way to identify the body of her furtive, thieving husband.

After the pre-credit sequence the movie opens with the dramatic demolition of a large public building (and ends in similar fashion). Just as Atlantic City, once 'the lungs of Philadelphia', seeks to rise from the rubble and emulate Las Vegas as a racketeer's paradise, so Lou Pasco (Burt Lancaster) an aged, impoverished numbers runner looks back wistfully to the stylish days of gangsters and personality, and re-creates them by successfully taking on the corporate world of drug-dealing. Lou survives and flourishes through redemptive violence. By killing the vicious thugs from Philadelphia he lives up to his own publicity, 'I'm dangerous. People come to me from Las Vegas.' The link between man and city is made visually: the block where Lou lives is scheduled for destruction and replacement by a casino, so a billboard on an outside wall announces, 'Atlantic City, you're back on the map. Again.' One important function performed by Lou, a watcher and voyeur, is to connect and relate selected parts of the city: the Boardwalk, the apartment building, the casino.

It is under the Boardwalk, among the rats and weeds in the domain of the homeless, that the protagonist of *Casino Moon* Anthony Russo kills another Italian-American, the action which precipitates him, in his words, 'away from the person I wanted to be'. Apart from the older generation of grotesque mobsters, consigned to history by their inability to infiltrate the casino hotels, the characters in *Casino Moon*, nourish their illusions of success. Mike, Anthony's father dreams of a golden casino. Elijah, the ex-middle weight champion of the world still fights to build up his investments. And Rosemary, once a bar dancer and occasional hooker, imagines herself with her daughter in Seattle attending 'afternoon teas in bright solariums'. Signs and billboards entice the punters with such slogans as: TAKE A CHANCE, DREAMS COME TRUE AT OUR SLOTS, and the Casino moon, a bright neon sign hanging over Bally's Grand, appears to outface nature itself.

Nostalgia pervades the atmosphere of the coastal city,'the place where all the old robber barons, industrial leaders and flappers from the 1920s used to come and sun themselves.' During the subsequent years of stagnation the Queen of Resorts continued to encourage hopes of a change of fortune:

> 'It's Atlantic City,' I remember [my father] saying. 'Anything could happen here.' And even in those ghost town years, ... there was a special feeling about the place. Something about the way the sea met the sky as the salt air rustled the red-and-white tents on the beach. Summer always seemed right around the corner.[2]

Rosemary knows her Seattle vision is merely a fantasy and settles for survival – 'with part of yourself intact'. Anthony who borrows money to promote Elijah's comeback fight believes there is 'some other kind of life out there', but fails to escape from the unyielding cage of Atlantic City whose landscape includes pawn shops, video retail outlets and vacant lots as well as Caesar's Palace. As he drives through side streets to his personal destiny, he reflects upon his brief career. 'All the houses seemed to be low, gray, and falling apart. No matter how much I struggled and hustled, it seemed I hadn't really gone anywhere. Every turn brought me back to Florida Avenue or Georgia Avenue, or one of these other ugly little blocks.'[3] The determinism is reinforced by the Boardwalk along which he is taken by police car after another shooting. Earlier he misread a sign as REDEMPTION CENTER; in Atlantic City the only act of redemption is changing quarters into dollars.

A more interesting urban case study is furnished by the fastest growing metropolis in the USA, Las Vegas. A convergence of casino/ hotel, theme park and shopping mall, it has combined the modernist concept of city as commercial spectacle with the postmodernism of entertainment and fantasy sites and spaces. The neon signs which for Tom Wolfe once constituted the essence of Las Vegas were aimed at motorists on Route 91. But now they attract middle aged, Middle America consumers to a pedestrian environment. Yet the industrialisation of gambling has turned the casinos of Las Vegas with their ubiquitous surveillance systems into prisons. Beyond the simulations of Ancient Rome and pirate ships lie back alleys, poverty and the homeless. With its water table continuously depleted the city sinks a few inches each year and seems, like Los Angeles, both a candidate for a Biblical catastrophe and a rich subject for crime fiction.

The artifice of Las Vegas is no utopia. In the USA generally the division of the city territorially into social and ethnic villages, linked economically but not culturally, inhibits urban recovery. This view has recently been supported by the sophisticated compu-terised techniques of space syntax which has found that the practice of dis-integration, the segregation of estates to exclude strangers and create a sense of local community has damaging consequences. 'Crime ... is partly the fault of inaccessible public spaces divided into segregated areas that freeze out natural movement.'[4] Con-versely, it has been demonstrated that the crime rate in American cities is reduced, as participation in city life increases.

In the segregated space of Double Deuce in Boston, which provides the title of Robert B. Parker's 1992 novel, even black cops patrol in pairs. The project is controlled by drug barons and by gangs, such as the Hobart Street Raiders, motivated by the needs that a capitalist society creates and stimulates. Towards the end of *Double Deuce*, Parker contextualises the ghetto geographically and sociologically. His description focuses upon the Fenway, part of an extended stretch of green space on the shores of the Charles River, which provides the Afro-American and Hispanic gangs with a playground. F. L. Olmsted who designed it in the nineteenth century called it the emerald necklace. 'It was a democratic green space and it remained pleasant through democratic shifts which moved the necklace in and out of bad neighbourhoods.'[5] Despite the graffiti at Fenway Stadium, the region with its colleges and Museum of Fine Arts proposes an urban alternative to Double Deuce whose young inhabitants Spenser nevertheless still considers to be doomed.

The modern city stands at the crossroads of space and time and is the expression of values that can be imagined and represented. Yet it is reviled from the right which fears mass society and the prospects for anarchy and revolution, and from the left which excoriates the capitalist inequalities that produce sweatshops and slums. Moreover, as cynical weariness and loss of moral certainties pervade hard-boiled narratives, 'an unanalysed incorporation of the 'noir' version of the city in left political consciousness disarms the left when it comes to critical examination of urban problems'.[6] This perception produces the question: do 'noir' crime fiction and images of decline encourage the acceptance of social responsibilities and the search for social justice?

Audiences may subjectify the crime narrative as a fantasy of risk and opportunity in a low-life milieu. The detective and *flâneur* often sympathise with similarly marginalised figures. But their own financial dependence on society makes them cynical and ironic rather than oppositional and generally ambivalent towards the city. The artist/*flâneur* is disappointed to find the promised urban pleasures withheld. This is the condition also of the PI or cop in LA (the last site for the American dream), a condition manifested in texts by Mosley and Ellroy as masculinity in crisis. Dissatisfaction is often compounded by the outcome of investigations which may be inconclusive and leave the status quo intact. The fragmented city, where experience can become dreamlike and insubstantial, yields greater or lesser pieces of fictions to the seeker after truth, bewildered by both the labyrinths and open spaces of the city.

The discourse of decline,in fiction, can be traced to the late nineteenth century Darwinist plots of Hardy, Dreiser and Zola in which the species survives at the expense of the individual. Even when large, industrial cities were flourishing, for instance in the 1920s, the language of decay persisted. It is in the metropolitan configuration that capitalism's spatial organisations have been most prominent so that the rhetoric of decline has been seized upon to express the broader anxieties and grievances of modern mass society. The city has consequently become the scapegoat for the general failings of the state. 'It is the "decline" of society that is sited in the cities. Thus urban decline will endure as long as the tensions and conflicts of society remain unresolved.'[7]

In this respect and others the city is a map of the psyche or in Philip Fisher's phrase, 'the metonymy for our total system of desires'. The detective novel by its very nature, seeks to control criminality – unrestrained desire – through objective techniques of surveillance, tracking (mapping the city) and deduction. However the PI, traditionally self-effacing, cannot deny the demands and expectations of others or, in many examples, his/her own emotions. The frustration experienced by the investigator who uncovers only shards of knowledge derives from the supposition that meaning is to be found in *everything*. Once the city becomes regarded as pervasively and ominously meaningful, fragments become signs in a sinister text and the result (as demonstrated in *The Crying of Lot 49*) is paranoia. The Italian novelist Calvino refers to the city's 'thick coating of signs'; representations can only partially discover what lies underneath, what constitutes 'the naked city'.

In the urban debate, decline becomes intertwined with the issue of race, so that the perceived threat of violence and the fear of minorities generate a demand for 'law and order' in the city. The signifiers of minority experience – slums, poverty, welfare, drugs, crime – underpin the attribution of blame and the abandonment of the inner city to the marginalised. Furthermore, apparent changes in urban power arrangements, and the reduction of male control over the city's core are explained in terms of redefined gender situations and relations, not only within the realm of economics but as cultural constructions also. Literary female PIs filling a variety of sexual roles provide illustrations of this development. The priestlike expertise of males in the management of technology (cars, guns, etc,) is increasingly challenged by women cops, or 'gumshoes', as they become empowered by the resources of information technology.

One favoured image of the city is that of a web of systems of communications. It is the image of cyberspace with the difference that access to information is not determined by social class, gender or race. Its model is not that of a command structure but one which is parallel and flat, facilitating change from the bottom up. The text of Sandra Scoppettone's *Everything You Have Is Mine* (1991) uses the vocabulary of computer networks (bulletin boards, modems, baud rates) to register the cultural constraints placed on women. It also demonstrates the ability of the protagonist, PI Lauren Laurano, to supply her own crash course in computing as she hunts down a rapist. By way of contrast, the eponymous police officer in *Mallory's Oracle* (1994), and its successor *The Man Who Lied to Women* (1995), displays phenomenal talents as a hacker from an early age, graduating from the imitation of sound codes for international calls on the telephone network to the penetration of the Requisition Department's database. Subsequently up-to-date PCs and state of the art components regularly arrive for her at the NYPD which she visits after school. There are, however, alternative city/cyberspace analogies such as the marketplace and the jungle. The promise of democracy waits to be fulfilled and when it arrives it may bear a closer resemblance to anarchy.

In *Casino Moon*, Blauner illustrates Atlantic City's history of boom and bust. At the time when Anthony's real father, Michael Dillon, is talking about gleaming castles, the Boardwalk's spatial reality consists of decrepit hotels and smashed storefronts. With the announcement of state-licensed gambling Caesar's, the Taj Mahal and other exotic 'castles' begin to appear, too late for the murdered Dillon and, as the narrative reveals, for his son also. Decline, therefore, is simply part of the urban rhythm of growth and decay. While it is 'a preferred reading of the material world [and of the city] ... dominant readings never go completely unchallenged; resistance is always possible.'[8] In other words, decline which, as a preferred reading, becomes a sort of urban essentialism is neither inevitable nor permanent. As centres of physical and intellectual energy and of national traditions, as sources of visual drama, as sites of the law and of politics (the term derives from *polis*, the ancient Greek city-state), cities retain a profound cultural and social magnitude.

'As a spatial frame, the street has a central value in city experience ... [which lies in] its qualities of the accidental and temporary, its invitation to a varied and multiple attention, its courting of adventure and interruption.'[9] Free movement in the street is constrained by an urban network of controls, while lower-class street life, boisterous and intrusive, may suffer ideological interpretation without explanation, its homeless, its hustlers and its harlots seen as an offence to the middle classes. In movies (notably Hitchcock's) this threat is often transferred to public spaces with the criminal invading one of the centres of bourgeois cultural capital: theatres, museums, monuments.

Through economic developments, migrations and the innovations of technology the industrial city of the 1980s completed the mutation from its nineteenth century version. As a consequence the street and its mysteries became overwhelmed by commodification. The bland, placeless complexes of buildings known as Edge Cities are defined by the absence of urban characteristics: public transport, architectural coherence, street fronts and street activity. Their spaces are 'single-minded', conceived to serve one purpose only. With the city remade for spectacle and consumption, the components of postmodern urban discourse have emerged as, on the one hand, eclectic architecture, gentrification, retail and festival marketplaces, and on the other, new ethnic patterns, homelessness, drug culture, cheap labour for service industries and the disappearance of civic concern and control. Developments in technology and their assimilation by crime fiction have been acknowledged earlier. Ridley Pearson's *No Witnesses* (1994) set in Seattle provides a further example of a rapidly increasing trend: the narrative is actuated by a psychopath who faxes extortion letters from an untraceable laptop and retrieves ransoms electronically from automatic cash machines.

The response of Bruce Mazlich to these momentous shifts and changes has been to claim, in *Conceptualizing Global History*, that 'global life, not the metropolitan, is now where the action is ... The city as adventure may be a thing of the past.'[10] This announcement ignores the globalisation of cities into cosmopolitan organisms where all parts of the world assume a co-presence and the creation of new global cities like Miami and Singapore, the world's first digital economy. As far as the crime text is concerned, reproduction of the city is not a direct, unmediated reflection of its material reality. Joe Gores has complained that hard-boiled novels continue to be written as though the USA is still in the 1930s or 1940s.

A similar conservatism is found in crime novels located in global capitals outside America. The sardonic, whiskey-drinking narrator of *Dance, Dance, Dance* by Haruki Murakami (1994) undergoes dizzying journeys in contemporary Tokyo, but the period is confused by the wisecracks, paranoia and mysterious women of the hard-boiled text. P. D. James's *Original Sin* (1994), set in and around a mock-Venetian, marble-encrusted palazzo on the banks of the river Thames is more precisely retrospective. Staring at the thick, muddy waters, James's characters recall the evidence of London's severe past of crime and punishment: Traitors' Gate; suffocating convict-hulks at Gravesend; and pirates hanged at Wapping Old Stairs. Similarly the brutal yet romantic books of Derek Raymond evoke both the sensibility of American pulp fiction writers as well as the wrecked landscapes of London after World War II. Raymond's city is populated by the desperate, by boozers, villains, tarts and bohemians. It features cheap bedsitters and persistent rain, and is suffused by *film noir* tensions and pathologies.

Answering the need for innovation in popular culture, the hard-boiled formula has frequently demonstrated its portability. An important consequence has been the emergence of the rural crime novel which takes place in bayous, hilly regions or desert country, challenging the form's traditional populism, an ideology which, despising mass society, abhorred the artificial, corrupt city (while celebrating small-town life and Nature, the map of God). It has found an echo in the phenomenon of 'noir' road movies (*True Romance, Kalifornia*) introduced at the end of 'Cinema Cities'.

Comparing his materials with those of Chandler, James Crumley identifies 'his dark streets in LA, my twisted highways in the mountain west'. In texts by Crumley and others such as Bill Pronzini, city plots, anxieties and moralities are stencilled upon the non-urban world. The actions of international arms cartels and the dumping of toxic materials constitute the crimes in *Dancing Bear* (1984), a narrative which begins and ends with images of garbage. Landfills and floating incinerators enable Jewels, the principal criminal, to grow rich on junk, sell drugs and pollute America. Like their equally battered and troubled urban counterparts, Crumley's investigators are lied to, deceived and even betrayed. Meriwether, Montana, the small town in *Dancing Bear* (and *The Wrong Case*) is scarred by both industrialisation and recession. Smelting stacks produce yellow smoke and a grimy sky smelling of 'cat piss and rotten eggs', but the lumber saws have been silenced and the pulp mills are on half shifts. A rash of tract housing spreads across the hill slopes.

The dusty bars, truck-stop cafés and seedy motels of Montana, Colorado and Wyoming and their rowdy customers impart a Western, honky-tonk flavour to Crumley's novels in which certain urban issues such as ethnic prejudice do not arise. In the film *The Last Seduction* (1993), the black detective Harlan cannot resist Bridget Gregory's sex talk that trades in racist stereotypes; it is a weakness that proves fatal. Their confrontation occurs in Beston, New York State ('Home of the Bulldogs') where Gregory is holed up after hoisting the proceeds from her husband's drug deal. A monstrous contemporary version of the classic 'noir' woman she uses her sexuality for psychological advantage and material gain. Greedy, foul-mouthed, in-your-face, Gregory possesses the confidence to flaunt her urban sophistication as she orders a Manhattan at a local bar. In addition she internalises the city, choosing the name WENDY KROY based on the mirror image of the words NEW YORK. 'Don't fuck with my image', she warns, and the clothes she wears – stockings and a short skirt, a mannish pin-stripe suit – are a further assertion of her contemptuous power. In this stylised cinematic product the small town in its triteness becomes a stage set for Gregory's wicked games and the intertextuality of Steve Barancik's script.

Early 'noir' texts while focusing upon menace, fear and avarice acknowledged that the city had a dark side which did not diminish its vitality and strength, and that from the start of the modern period dangerous excitement had been part of the city's appeal. Drawn to the metropolis (and crime) as spectacle, the cinema rapidly showed its ability to portray the vibrancy of the city in images of great power, and to move around it capturing a sense of both urban incarnations and transformations. In its romanticism the cinema has at least avoided the routine contempt for the urban scene which has been a recurrent feature of modern western literature, especially in the late nineteenth and twentieth centuries. Commenting on Patrick Keiller's film *London* (1994), Ian Sinclair attributes the city's silence and loss of resonance to 'a conspiracy of the suburbs, an attack on metropolitan life and all its amenities by small-minded provincials, careerists distrustful of the liberties of the café-bar, the aimlessness of the flâneur.'[11]

The metropolis is embraced by wanderers, poets and dreamers; relevant American cities include Los Angeles (segregated and militarised but still the home of Hollywood) and the gambling towns such as Atlantic City. Fictional detectives stay committed to the idea of urban society and the chance of its redemption. Paco Taibo's Mexico City detective Hector Belascoarán Shayne describes himself as just another *mexicano* trying to make it in the Mexico jungle, but he turns the daily variety of city life into a practical resource. Shayne uses as secretaries a plumber, an upholsterer and an engineer who keep him in touch with 'the real Mexico'. Hector's association with these other craftsmen – he acknowledges his skills and experience are inferior – establishes his normality, protecting him against 'the myth of the super-detective with its cosmopolitan and exotic delusions'. The arrangement is a democratic one with Hector obliged to 'quote prices on the repair of Naugahyde love seats or broken faucets, and every now and then, take a message from the engineer's girlfriend'.[12]

Deyan Sudjic in *The 100 Mile City* refers to the mistaken vision of cities in the twentieth century as having fallen from grace. De Certeau with his belief in the everyday never entertained that vision, believing that while capitalist society represses it does not destroy the creativity of the people. The shape and spaces of the city are at the forefront of intellectual debate, sustained by a new responsiveness to the attraction and liveliness of urban variety and disarray. The future of the city – in the USA and elsewhere – will depend not only on economics and politics but also on geography, language and art, on a debate whose terms ought to include 'participation and democracy', 'ecology and nature', and 'space and design'.

Crime fiction cannot avoid the reproduction of negative images but they may co-exist textually with utopian longings. Furthermore, the preceding examination demonstrates that redemption, the empowerment of the marginalised, the success of the underdog, even redistribution of wealth are all constitutive of the genre. What it owes the city is the imagination to create projections that transcend the rhetoric of inevitable decline and the bourgeois mystifications of the 'tragic sense of life'. The wisdom taught by the fairy tale, Walter Benjamin asserted, was that the forces of the mythical world should be met with cunning and high spirits; it is a lesson which has a place in the discourse of urban crime fiction.

NOTES

1   R. B. Parker, *The Widening Gyre* (Wallington, Severn House, 1991), p. 153.

2   P. Blauner, *Casino Moon* (London, Viking, 1994), pp. 32, 33.

3   *Ibid.*, p. 244.

4   Fisher, 'Zooming in on danger zones', *The Guardian (Online)*, 12 January, 1995, 4.

5   R. B. Parker, *Double Deuce* (London, Penguin, 1993), p.195.

6   D. MacCannell , 'Democracy's Turn: On Homeless Noir', in J. Copjec, *Shades of Noir*, p. 280.

7   R. A. Beauregard, *Voices of Decline: The Postwar Fate of American*

Cities (Oxford, UK, Cambridge, USA, Blackwell, 1993), p. 323.

8   Jackson, *Maps of Meaning* (London, Unwin Hyman, 1989), p. 186.

9   P. Fisher, *Hard Facts: Setting and Form in the American Novel* (Oxford and New York, Oxford University Press, 1987), p.135.

10 Quoted in B. Mazlich, 'The Flâneur from Spectator to Representation' in K. Tester (ed.), *The Flâneur* (London and New York, Routledge, 1994), p. 56.

11 I. Sinclair, 'Necropolis of Fretful Ghosts', *Sight and Sound*, 4:6 (June 1994), 14.

12 P. I. Taibo II, *An Easy Thing* (trans. W. I. Neuman, New York, Viking), p. 67.

SELECT BIBLIOGRAPHY

All works cited in the 'Select bibliography' are printed with the publication dates of the latest editions. In some cases the author has used earlier editions of these works for reference in text. The dates of publication to these editions are given both in text and in the 'Notes' at the end of each chapter.

PRIMARY

Abella, A. (1992), *The Killing of the Saints*, London and New York, Serpent's Tail.

Auster, P. (1988), *City of Glass* in *The New York Trilogy*, London, Faber.

Blauner, P. (1994), *Casino Moon*, London, Viking.

Burke, J. L. (1989), *The Neon Rain*, London, Mysterious Press.

—— (1991), *A Morning for Flamingos*, New York, Avon Books.

Cain, J. M. (1985), *The Five Great Novels*, London, Picador.

Cain, P. (1987), *Fast One*, Harpenden, No Exit Press.

Campbell, R. (1993), *Boneyards*, New York, Pocket Books.

Chandler, R. (1971), *The Big Sleep*, Harmondsworth, Penguin.

—— (1975), *Farewell, My Lovely*, Harmondsworth, Penguin.

—— (1952), *The Lady in the Lake*, Harmondsworth, Penguin.

Charyn, J. (1984), *The Isaac Quartet*, London, Zomba Books.

Constantine, K. C. (1986), *Always a Body to Trade*, London, Allison and Busby.

Crumley, J. (1984), *Dancing Bear*, New York, Vintage.

Demarco, G. (1984), *October Heat*, London, Pluto Press.

Dunne, J. G. (1978), *True Confessions*, New York, Pocket Books.

Gores, J. (1972), *Dead Skip*, New York, Random House.

—— (1993), *Gone, No Forwarding*, New York, Mysterious Press.

Hall, J. (1989), *Under Cover of Daylight*, London, Mandarin.

Hammett, D. (1975), *Red Harvest*, London, Pan.

—— (1975), *The Maltese Falcon*, London, Pan.

—— (1977), *The Big Knockover and Other Stories*, Harmondsworth, Penguin.

Hiassen, C. (1987), *Tourist Season*, New York, Warner Books.

—— (1989), *Double Whammy*, New York, Warner Books.

Himes, C. (1985), *A Rage in Harlem (For Love of Imabelle)*, London, Allison and Busby.

—— (1974), *Cotton Comes to Harlem*, Harmondsworth, Penguin.

—— (1969), *The Heat's On*, London, Panther.

—— (1990), *Run Man Run*, London, Allison and Busby.

Hoyt, R. (1993),   *Marimba*, New York, Tor Books.

Koenig, J. (1989), *Floater*, Harmondsworth, Penguin.

Leonard, E. (1984), *Stick*, Harmondsworth, Penguin.

—— (1985), *LaBrava*, Harmondsworth, Penguin.

—— (1991), *Get Shorty*, New York, Dell.

Lochte, D. (1994), *Blue Bayou*, New York, Ivy Books.

McBain, E. (1989), *Downtown*, London and New York, Guild Publishing.

Mosley, W. (1991), *Devil in a Blue Dress*, London, Serpent's Tail.

—— (1992), *A Red Death*, New York, Pocket Books.

—— (1993), *White Butterfly*, New York, Pocket Books.

O'Connell, C. (1995), *Mallory's Oracle*, London, Arrow.

Paretsky, S. (1992), *Killing Orders* in *Indemnity Only and Killing Orders*, London, Victor Gollancz.

—— (1990), *Toxic Shock*, London, Penguin.

—— (1991), *Burn Marks*, New York, Dell.

—— (1992), *Guardian Angel*, London, Penguin.

Parker, R. B. (1991), *The Widening Gyre*, Wallington, Severn House.

—— (1993), *Double Deuce*, London, Penguin.

Percy, W. (1961), *The Moviegoer*, New York, Popular Library.

Puzo, M. (1970), *The Godfather*, New York, Fawcett.

Pynchon, T. (1967), *The Crying of Lot 49*, New York, Bantam.

Roberts, L. (1990), *Pepper Pike*, London, Coronet,.

—— (1992), *Deep Shaker*, New York, St Martin's.

Sallis, J. (1992), *The Long-Legged Fly*, New York, Avon Books.

Sanchez, T. (1992), *Hollywoodland (Zoot Suit Murders)*, London, Methuen.

Schulman, S. (1984), *The Sophie Horowitz Story*, Tallahassee, Naiad.

—— (1986), *Girls, Visions and Everything*, Seattle, The Seal Press.

Scoppettone, S. (1992), *Everything You Have is Mine*, London, Virago.

Shames, L. (1992), *Florida Straits*, New York, Dell.

Smith, J. (1992), *Tourist Trap*, New York, Ivy Books.

—— (1990), *New Orleans Mourning*, New York, Ivy Books.

Taibo II, P. I. (1990), *An Easy Thing*, New York, Viking.

Vachss, A. (1990), *Hard Candy*, New York, Signet.

Willeford, C. (1985), *Miami Blues*, New York, Ballantine.

Wiltz, C. (1991), *The Emerald Lizard*, New York, Dutton.

Wolfe, T. (1988), *The Bonfire of the Vanities*, London, Picador.

SECONDARY

Anderson, K. J., The Idea of Chinatown: The Power of Place and Institutional Practice in the Making of a Racial Category, *Annals of the Association of American Geographers*, 77 (1987), 580–98.

Atkinson, M., 'Crossing the Frontiers', *Sight and Sound*, 4:1 (January 1994), 14–17.

Babener, L., 'Murder in New Orleans', *Clues*, 10:2 (Fall/Winter 1989), 1–20.

Beauregard, R. A., *Voices of Decline: The Postwar Fate of American Cities*, Oxford, UK and Cambridge, USA, Blackwell, 1993.

Bentley, C., 'Radical Anger: Dashiell Hammett's *Red Harvest*', in B. Doherty (ed.), *American Crime Fiction: Studies in the Genre*, London, Macmillan, 1988.

Berman, M., *All That Is Solid Melts Into Air: The Experience of Modernity*, London, Verso, 1983.

Bryan, V. H., 'Land of Dreams: Image and Reality in New Orleans', *Urban Resources* 1 (Spring 1984), 29–35.

Cavin, S., 'On the Voodoo Trail to Jazz', *Journal of Jazz Studies*, 3:1 (Fall 1975), 4–27.

Cawelti, J. G., *Adventure, Mystery, and Romance: Formula Stories as Art and Popular Culture*, Chicago, University of Chicago Press, 1976.

Christianson, S. R., 'Tough Talk and Wisecracks: Language as Power in American Detective Fiction', *Journal of Popular Culture*, 23:2 (Fall 1989), 151–62.

Clarens, C., *Crime Movies: from Griffith to the Godfather and Beyond*, London, Secker and Warburg, 1980.

Clarke, G., (ed.), *The American City: Literary and Cultural Perspectives*, London, Vision Press, 1988.

Conrad, P., *The Art of the City*, Oxford and New York, Oxford University Press, 1984.

Copjec, J., (ed.), *Shades of Noir*, London and New York, Verso, 1993.

Davis, M., *City of Quartz: Excavating the Future in Los Angeles*, London, Vintage, 1990.

De Certeau, M., 'Practices of Space', in M. Blonsky (ed.), *On Signs*, Oxford, Blackwell, 1985.

——, 'Walking in the City', in S. During (ed.), *The Cultural Studies Reader*, London and New York, Routledge, 1993.

Fine, D., (ed.), *Los Angeles in Fiction*, Albuquerque, University of New Mexico Press, 1984.

Fisher, P., *Hard Facts: Setting and Form in the American Novel*, Oxford and New York, Oxford University Press, 1987.

Foucault, M., 'Of Other Spaces', *diacritics* 16:1 (Spring 1986), 22–27.

Geoghegan, T., 'Chicago, Pride of the Rustbelt', *The New Republic*, 25 March 1985, 18–23.

Gregory, S., *Private Investigations: The Novels of Dashiell Hammett*, Carbondale, Southern Illinois University Press, 1985.

Gross, L., 'Film Aprés Noir', *Film Comment*, 12:4 (July/August 1976), 44–5.

Harvey, D., *The Condition of Postmodernity*, Oxford, Blackwell, 1989.

Herron, D., *The Dashiell Hammett Tour*, San Francisco, City Lights Books, 1991.

Horwell, V., 'Sister Gumshoe', *Weekend Guardian*, 25–6 April 1992, 15.

Humm, M., 'Feminist Detective Fiction', in C. Bloom (ed.), *Twentieth-Century Suspense: The Thriller Comes of Age*, Basingstoke and London, Macmillan, 1990, 237–54.

Jackson, P., 'Street life: the politics of Carnival', *Society and Space*, 6 (1988), 213–27.

Jarvis, B., 'Crime in the "City of Glass": The Case for a Postmodern Detective Story', *Over Here*, 10:2 (Winter 1980), 34–44.

Kael, P., *Deeper Into Movies*, London, Calder and Boyars, 1975.

Koolhaas, R., *Delirious New York: A Retroactive Manifesto for Manhattan*, New York, Oxford University Press, 1979.

Langer, P., 'Four Images of Organized Diversity: Bazaar, Jungle, Organism and Machine', in L. Rodwin and R. M. Hollister (eds.), *Cities of the Mind: Images and Themes in the Social Sciences*, New York and London, Plenum Press, 1984, 97–118.

Marcus, S., 'Dashiell Hammett and the Continental Op', *Partisan Review*, XLI: 3 (1974), 362–77.

Mazzoleni, D., 'The City and the Imaginary', *New Formations*, 11 (Subjects in Space, Summer 1990).

Muller, G.H., *Chester Himes*, Boston, Twayne Publishers, 1989.

/Munt/ S./ (ed.), *New Lesbian Criticism: Literary and Cultural Readings*, New York and London, Harvester Wheatsheaf, 1992.

Nelson, R., 'Domestic Harlem: the Detective Fiction of Chester Himes', *Virginia Quarterly Review*, 48:2 (Spring 1972), 260–76.

Penman, I., 'Juke Box and Johnny Boy', *Sight and Sound*, 3:4 (April 1993), 10–11.

Prendergast, C., *Paris and the Nineteenth Century*, Oxford UK and Cambridge USA, Blackwell, 1992.

Pye, M., *Maximum City: the Biography of New York*, London, Picador, 1993.

Reed, I., *Shrovetide in Old New Orleans*, Garden City, New York, Doubleday, 1978.

Reid, D., *Sex, Death and God in LA*, New York, Pantheon, 1992.

Rieff, D., *Los Angeles: Capital of the Third World*, London, Phoenix, 1993.

Schrader, P., 'Notes on Film Noir', *Film Comment*, 8:1 (Spring, 1972), 8–13.

Sharpe, W. and Wallock, L., (eds.), *Visions of the Modern City: Essays in History, Art and Literature*, Baltimore and London, The Johns Hopkins University Press, 1987.

Sibley, D., *Geographies of Exclusion: Society and Difference in the West*, London, Routledge, 1995.

Sigal. C., 'The lure of the mean streets', *Guardian Review*, 17 June 1988, 25.

Sinclair, I., 'Necropolis of Fitful Ghosts', *Sight and Sound*, 4:6 (June 1994), 12–15.

Sparks, R., *Television and the drama of crime: moral tales and the place of crime in public life*, Buckingham and Philadelphia, Open University Press, 1992.

Sudjic, D., *The 100 Mile City*, London, Andre Deutsch, 1992.

Tester, K., (ed.), *The Flâneur*, London and New York, Routledge, 1994.

Thomson, D., *America in the Dark*, London, Hutchinson, 1978.

Uricchio, W., and Pearson, R. E., 'I'm Not Fooled by That Cheap Disguise', in Uricchio and Pearson (eds.), *The Many Lives of the Batman*, London and New York, BFI/Routledge, 1991, 182–213.

Vidler, A., *The Architectural Uncanny*, Cambridge, Mass., MIT Press, 1992.

Willett, R., *Hard-Boiled Fiction*, Halifax, BAAS/Ryburn, 1992.

Williams, J., *Into the Badlands: a Journey Through the American Dream*, London, Paladin, 1991.

Winokur, M., 'Eating Children is Wrong', *Sight and Sound*, 1:7 (November 1991), 10–13.

Zukin, S., *Landscapes of Power: From Detroit to Disney World*, Berkeley, University of California Press, 1991.

——, *The Culture of Cities*, Oxford, Blackwell, 1995.

INDEX

Main page references are indicated in bold. Entries in italics are novels unless otherwise indicated.